Contents

The Whole Book

The Problems

D1206580

Preface

This book is designed to supplement problem-solving oriented mathematics curricula in the middle grades and beyond. The tasks assume high standards for student performance, communication, and understanding of mathematical ideas. And these tasks are designed for groups: they provide a structure for learning to work together.

Over the last decade, many teachers have discovered how wonderful it is to unbolt the desks from the floor and push them into groups. Students have become more accustomed to working together in math instead of working alone. Research has advanced our understanding of what happens in groups and how group work helps children learn. And some new curriculum materials even come with frequent suggestions for group problems and projects.

How did this happen? We first saw problems like these—you cut up the page and pass out the clues—in the Humboldt County, California *Green Box* materials. They called them *six-bit* problems, because every problem had six clues. The *Green Box* inspired books such as *Get It Together* and *Group Solutions* (from the Lawrence Hall of Science), and the *Cooperative Problem Solving* Series (from Creative Publications). Today (in 1996) millions of students are now familiar with this format. Of course, cooperative learning goes far beyond six-bit problems. There have also been many projects, publications, inservice programs, and workshops on all aspects of group work in mathematics. Most important, teachers have talked to teachers, and have learned from one another that what once would have been an un-thinkable invitation to chaos is in fact an unparalleled chance to help our students become responsible, independent learners.

This book has more than 100 new problems. If you have done some cut-up-the-page-and-pass-out-clues problems in your class, this book will look familiar. We hope it has a playful spirit and engaging ideas. But this book makes some assumptions about the students. While there are some good "starters" in this book, most of these problems assume that students already have some experience working together in groups.

Since today's students are more experienced, these problems can be bigger and deeper. Some of these problems will extend "beyond the bells"—they may take more than one period, or they may turn into problems-of-the-week (POWs) or other homework. Some of the problems are mathematically quite challenging as well, but remember: when groups work well, the group can solve problems the individuals cannot handle alone. As one field-test teacher said, "If I can't figure it out myself, I have to give it to the kids."

This book also focuses on particular mathematical ideas. The problems are organized into four categories. Three are clearly content: *Patterns*, *Spatial*, and *Proportion*. The fourth is structural: *Open*, as in "open-ended." They overlap, of course: similar triangles are *Spatial*, but they live in the *Proportion* category in this book. A *Patterns* problems with many solutions might dwell in the *Open*.

Acknowledgements

In return for food, a dedicated group of teachers tested these problems: Annie Alcott, Harold Asturias, Julie Bagniefski, Pam Beck, Julie Crozier, Cynthia Davis, Mishaa DeGraw, Barry Fike, Donna Goldenstein, Susie Goodin, Duane Habecker, Natalia Jacopetti, Vicky Luibrand, Michelle Millard, Wendy Revelli, Barbara Shulgold, Teresa Stasio, and Jean Stenmark. Special thanks go to Bob Whitlow and Aurora School in Oakland, California, for encouragement and use of the space for those problem-testing dinners.

Another group tested many of these problems in classrooms under a very tight time schedule: Patty Armstrong, Karen Baum, René Beradi, Mark Butler, April Cherrington, Cindy deClercq, Kathleen Davies, Kris Ellingson, Tamara Evans, John Everett, Tom Frizzi, Marti Hartrick, Valerie Henry, Susan Hoffmier, Mary Sue Kennedy, Sue Kinder, Cheryl Lilhanand, Ford Long, Carole Maples, Charlotte Meade, Nancy Morton, Barbara Moser, Ingrid Oyen, Carol Piercy, Alice Spier, Barry Sullivan, Jeff Trubey, and Karen Vipond. Many of these teachers are involved with the California Mathematics Renaissance, a project that has done a great deal to improve mathematics education in the middle grades. Judy Mumme, Carole Maples, Teferi Messeret, and Mardi Gale of the Renaissance helped recruit field-test teachers and gave valuable advice. In addition to the teachers, we thank the students, who worked hard and gave conscientious and valuable feedback.

Others helped in diverse ways. Merle Silverman of Dale Seymour Publications first convinced us this book could be created and, more important, distributed. Ruth Cossey and Vicky Webber helped fill us in on recent progress in research and practice. Yvonne Judice of McDonald's Corporation gave us permission to use data from their annual report. Kate Spelman of Steinhart & Falconer, San Francisco, helped to navigate the legal thickets.

Of course, none of this would have been possible without the support of EQUALS staff past and present. We particularly thank Virginia Thompson and Nancy Kreinberg, and members of the EQUALS "Writers' Block" for help with some prose: Louise Lang, Terri Belcher, Karen Mayfield, Grace Dávila Coates, and, of course, Aunt Jean.

Meg Holmberg and Anne Erickson kept me well-supported and mostly sane, respectively. Meg helped with inventing problems and smoothing the words, and with countless other necessities such as childcare and paying the bills even though she was in the middle of a big project too. Anne played SimAnt with me, played catch and kitchen soccer, helped bring food to the testing meetings, and made many suggestions for problems, including *Triple Crown*.

How We Made This Book

Technology has come a long way in the last few years. If we thought about it, many of us writers and publishers would acknowledge in every book the genius of "the two Steves"—Jobs and Wozniak, without whom few of us would point or click—for making it possible.

The book was created on a Power Macintosh 7100. We used Microsoft Word 5.1a for the text and MacDraw Pro for the original problems. Eventually the problems found their way into PageMaker. Technical drawings are in Claris Draw and Adobe Illustrator. The Hawaii sectional (page 137) was scanned on an Apple Color OneScanner and touched up in Adobe Photoshop. We made the blocks on pages 102–105 using Virtus VR.

Rose Craig created the line drawings directly in Illustrator using a pressure-sensitive Wacom graphics tablet. (Sally Noll, bless her, used gouache on Bristol board for the front cover. *Something* was real.) We put everything but the cover together using PageMaker 6.0 and 6.5, and printed page proofs on an Apple LaserWriter 16/600PS, which is one great printer. The heads are Lubalin Demi and the text is mostly Minion.

Coleen Connell, Bill Washburn, and the staff of George Lithograph of Brisbane, California shepherded the book through the printing process. They took the SyQuest and Zip cartridges and turned them into bound books in two weeks. Awesome.

Tim Erickson
Oakland, California
November, 1995
July, 1997

Introduction

This is a collection of math problems designed to complement a high-standards middle school curriculum (grades 6–8). Some of these problems are appropriate in fifth grade, and many will challenge even the most experienced high-school students.

This "breadth of usefulness" arises because these are problems for *groups* to solve together. There are many ways to solve them, many points of access. So while some hot-shot sophomores may be stumped or overwhelmed, eleven-year-olds who know how to work together will build a convincing solution—probably using much simpler mathematics.

Each problem comes on clue cards cut from a single sheet of paper. Students pass out the clues to the members of the group. Because each person's information is essential, everyone needs to work together to solve the problem. This format makes it easy for students to begin solving problems in groups, and it is particularly easy for teachers to manage. Of course, there is a great deal more to cooperative learning in mathematics than problems like these, but they are still a useful tool for teachers. And they're fun for the kids.

Resources

Get It Together is a collection of problems in this format from the same author. To order, call EQUALS at (510) 642-1910 or your favorite catalog.

Tim Erickson, 1989. *Get It Together: Math problems for groups, grades 4–12*. Berkeley: EQUALS Program, Lawrence Hall of Science.

We can't possibly do justice to the literature on cooperative learning, but all of the Big Thinkers contributed to the following, and it has an extensive resource list:

Neil Davidson, ed. 1990. *Cooperative Learning in Mathematics: A handbook for teachers*. Menlo Park: Addison-Wesley.

The next two are especially thoughtful and have recent new editions:

Elizabeth G. Cohen, 1994. *Designing Groupwork: Strategies for the heterogeneous classroom* (Second edition). New York: Teachers College Press.

Jeanne Gibbs, 1994. *Tribes: A new way of learning and being together*. Santa Rosa, CA: Center Source Systems.

Finally, these two are thought-provoking, and cogently question some of our closely-held assumptions:

Alfie Kohn, 1992. *No Contest: The case against competition*. Revised edition. New York: Houghton Mifflin.

Alfie Kohn, 1993. *Punished by Rewards: The trouble with gold stars, incentive plans, A's, praise, and other bribes*. New York: Houghton Mifflin.

Why Use Group Work in Mathematics?

The first time students do problems this way, they may be a little discombobulated. They may not understand at first that the *group* has a problem to solve. They may not understand that they're allowed—even required—to talk. But after a few problems, they start asking for more. Here are some of the benefits you might see:

- **Interest**: Almost all of the students are engaged almost all of the time.

- **Success**: Students in a group can solve harder and larger problems than the individuals can.

- **Multiple Approaches**: A student in a group may see several different approaches to a problem from different group members.

- **Peer Help**: Group members explain things to their colleagues quickly and effectively, without using up whole-class time.

- **Modalities**: Group work will reach some students when seat work and lecture will not.

- **Communication**: Students naturally use mathematical vocabulary as they work these problems. And even the most experienced student can learn to explain mathematical ideas more clearly.

- **Contributions from all**: Students you think of as weak or disruptive may surprise you with effective contributions to group work, and "strong" students may discover that "those other kids" know more than they thought.

- **Collaboration**: Working together well is a skill you can learn. Few schools teach it explicitly, so we need to teach it within the disciplines. Most jobs (including those in math-related fields) require it.

Group work can help you learn how your students are thinking. First, it's actually possible to keep track of eight groups solving problems as you walk around the class. You can give groups the "individual" attention and encouragement you can't always spare for each of thirty-two students. Second, because students are in groups, they have to communicate. That means that you can hear what they say and see what they write and watch how they organize data. You don't get this kind of information from quiet, individual seat work.

Group work in the math classroom lets students solve genuine problems in interesting situations. If the problems are complex but not impossible, students will persist, and success will be rewarding. Group work makes students mathematically limber, with many strategies at their disposal. Group work will help students see that *math* does not equal *alone*. "Being good at math" requires working together, explaining, and listening as well as calculating and knowing the Pythagorean Theorem. Finally, working together will make students stronger when they work alone: autonomous thinkers, free of the book, free of the teacher, and free to keep looking for answers.

Feedback

We would love to hear from you—what works, what doesn't, praise, complaints—the works. The best way to reach us is by electronic mail. Here is our address:

publications@eeps.com

We also have a web site. If your school does not have access yet, you district or county office may. We will post new information as it becomes available. And if you send us problems you or your students write (and you give us permission) we'll share them with the world through the Internet. Here's our URL:

http://www.eeps.com

And though we're a teeny home business, we do accept real letters and telephone calls.

eeps media
5269 Miles Avenue
Oakland, CA 94618-1044
voice and messages:
 (510) 653-3377 (653-EEPS)
fax:
 (510) 428-1120

A Quick Start

Preparation

Each problem lives on its own page. Photocopy the page of the problem you want the students to do (one for each group of four), cut the clues apart, and stuff the clues into envelopes (or just paper-clip them together). If the problem needs anything else—a map, say—have that copied as well. Any other material (blocks, beans, pencils, compasses, calculators, whatever) should be available.

If everything is ready, set up groups of four, explain the rules, and pass out the problems! Here are the rules:

The Rules

- Begin each problem by passing out clues to the members of your group.

- **You may not look at anyone else's clue**. You may share your own clue by reading it or telling others what's on it, *but you may not show it to anyone else*. (Special language needs change this, of course.)

- **If you have a question, check with your group first**. If your group agrees that no one in the group can answer the question, you may all raise your hands and the teacher will come. (You also raise your hands when you all agree that you're done with the problem.)

- **Be sure everybody participates**. You may have to decide what this means to you. It may simply mean that everybody gets to talk or to use the scissors; it could also mean everybody listens.

- When you're done, collect the clues and stuff them back into the envelope. Then raise your hands. The teacher will give you a new problem.

It's Your Call

Modify any suggestion in this book to fit your needs, and use your imagination to solve problems that these instructions don't cover. For example, what if you can't make groups of four? Then have some groups of three in which one person gets two clues. (Groups of three are often better than fives, because the individuals have more to do.) Other questions you have might be answered in the rest of these introductory pages.

Your First Time

Organizing students into groups will not make them cooperate. There are a gazillion different things to watch out for. You want to try this for the first time. What should you do?

Preview the problems.

Check the index and pick a good "Starter." Read the comments on the "cluster" page. *The first time you try this*, solve the problems you plan to do in class ahead of time—with a small cooperative group, if possible, but alone if necessary. Note words or ideas that may be hard for your students. As you and your students become more experienced, you'll still preview the problems, but you won't have to solve every one.

Prepare the materials.

Leave enough time to get things copied and cut. You might decide to let the students do the cutting and stuffing into envelopes.

Pick a grouping strategy.

Don't let students choose their own groups. We like random groups of four. We like the groups to last for longer than one class session, but not more than a couple weeks to a month. That way, everyone gets to work with many other people. Special language needs can alter this; see page 14.

You can make random groups by passing out playing cards (the kings go to this table, the sevens over there, and so forth).

Explain the rules and mechanics.

Students need to know what to do. Explain about passing out the clues and returning them to the envelopes. The rules are on page 8. Check to see that students understand them.

Do it!

As groups work, try to *interact* with groups (rather than *intervening* for individuals), and try not to give answers. See "Teacher's Role" beginning on page 20.

Hold a class discussion.

Be sure to listen. Let the students do the discussing. Here are some questions you might ask:

- Are you convinced you had the right answer? How did you convince yourselves?

- What was hardest about doing math in groups? What was easiest?

- Did everybody get a chance to talk?

- Did you learn any math from a member of your group?

Call on as many different groups and individuals as possible.

Reflect.

As soon as you have some time alone, think and write about what happened. How did the random groups work out? Did anything or anyone surprise you? What was the best idea a student had? How did the class handle the problems? Did they have trouble with the math? With collaborating? What will make it better next time? What did you learn about your students? A little reflection will help you in your planning.

About the Problems

This section describes how the problems are laid out on the page and how they're organized in this book. It's pretty straightforward.

Problems, Clusters, and Categories

Problems are grouped together into clusters of common mathematical ideas. Most clusters have about four problems. In general, the easier problems come first, the most challenging at the end.

Each cluster has an introductory page. This "cluster page" includes a list of materials and commentary for each problem in the cluster. It also includes questions to help students as they work on the problems or to nurture discussion afterwards.

The page numbers for each cluster appear on "bleed tabs." ("Bleeding" means being printed out to the edge of the page.) You can use these tabs to help you find clusters in the book, not unlike the tabs in most Yellow Pages®.

Clusters are, in turn, loosely grouped into four categories. In this book, the four categories are *Patterns*, *Open* (as in open-ended), *Spatial*, and *Proportions*. The richest problems naturally draw from more than one of these big ideas, but categories are still useful for finding problems whose main focus fits one of the four big ideas.

How the Problems Appear on the Page

We've put a problem on the facing page as an example. (You can use it in class, too.) Here are some things to notice:

- Every clue has the name of the problem on it. Near the title is a blip (e.g., ➤) which varies with position on the page. You can think of them as, "up, down, left, right." The titles and blips will help you sort the clues if sixty of them spill on the floor.

- Every problem has either four or six clues. *If the problem has six clues, clues ○ and △ (the two at the bottom) are optional.* It is possible to solve the problem without them. You can read more about optional clues on page 12.

- Some problems have small *labels* at the bottom of the page (for example, *Balloons* on page 77). The labels act as manipulatives, compass directions, etc. We think it is best for students to create their own labels, however, since that's part of the decision process.

- Any "double-sized" clue (it has a ❖) at the bottom of the page is for *the whole group* to read *before* the individuals work on their own clues. If you wish, you can withhold the individual clues until they've read and processed the group clue. (Example: *Sierpinski Bricks*, page 42.)

- Each page has a *keyword strip* along the bottom identifying broad content areas and special features (e.g., "POW," "Starter"). The name of the cluster appears as well. The keywords are indexed on pages 188–189.

▲ Red Square

The green square is 8 cm on a side.

Work with your group to make the figure and determine the area of a red square.

▼ Red Square

The blue circle fits exactly into the green square.

Work with your group to make the figure and determine the area of the red square.

◄ Red Square

You can just fit two identical orange circles into the blue circle.

Work with your group to make the figure and determine the area of the red square.

► Red Square

A red square just fits inside an orange circle.

Work with your group to make the figure and determine the area of the red square.

○ Red Square

Hint: If you can't see how to find the area of the red square, there are several strategies. One is to cut it along the diagonal to make two triangles (that diagonal will become the base of the triangles)—then add the areas of the two triangles together.

△ Red Square

Hint: If you can't see how to find the area of the red square, there are several strategies. One is to make an accurate full-sized drawing and measure it.

from *United We Solve*

Geometry, measurement, area, circles.

Cluster: none

More About the Problems

Optional Clues

When there are six clues, the bottom two ($\bigcirc$ and $\triangle$) are optional. There are several types of optional clues:

- clues that help confirm a solution;

- clues that give strategy hints (labeled **Hint:** in the problems); and

- clues that provide extensions to the problem (labeled **Extension:**).

You can use optional clues for groups of five or six students, but *it may be inappropriate or disruptive to hand out the "extensions" clues with the others.* If students have a hard time figuring out what they're supposed to do, the last thing they need is an extra task. Many teachers hold back all of the optional clues until a group has a question or is finished, at which time the optional clues come into play—to help the students over a "stuck" place or to help them check their work.

Materials

Many teachers organize these materials by putting all of the clues for a group into a labeled envelope. A set of ten envelopes (say) constitutes a class set you can use from year to year and share with other teachers.

Get as much help from the students as you can. When a group finishes a problem, have the students put the clues back into the envelope and put the envelope where it belongs. When they need extra materials—calculators, scissors, blocks, and so forth—be sure they're available so students can get them. Many teachers have a system in which one member of each group is allowed to get up and get materials; this keeps the number of people "up" under control.

Of course, students also need a clear space to work together. If you are blessed with tables, great. Have students put their backpacks away and you're ready to start. If you don't have tables, you can still shove individual desks together to make a common surface. It really helps if that surface is flat.

Note: for problems with four clues, the cut width of the clues (4 1/4 inches) is a little too wide to fit in a regular #10 envelope (4 1/8 inches). Just trim the long edges of the paper before you cut up the clues; you can lose a half inch off each side without cutting into the writing.

What Is the Task?

In some classes—especially classes new to group work—students may get into trouble because they don't know what they're supposed to accomplish.

To help, you may suggest that the group first decide what they're supposed to do or figure out. ("Your first task is to figure out what the task is.") You could let them know:

- In some problems, the task appears on every card.

- In some problems, the task appears only on some cards.

- In other problems, different tasks appear on different cards. In that case, the group should do them all.

Experienced groups will not need this help; it's part of what they have learned to do with every problem.

Types of products. These problems ask students to do various things. Ordinarily, "the task" is simply to agree on an answer. But sometimes, they have to build a structure or make a group display such as a graph.

You should alter the "product" the problems call for to suit your needs and your students' experience. For example, *Amityville Area* (page 139) asks for a scale drawing. You could relax that if your students are not ready for scale. Similarly, *Giant Basketball* (page 162) asks for just an answer. But you could tell the students they have to make a presentation about their group's work and write it up for their portfolios. Your call.

"Bigger" products (e.g., "group drawing") appear in the keyword strips.

Multiple Solutions

Many of these problems—especially those from the *Open* category—have multiple solutions. The keywords (in the strip at the bottom of the page) indicate which ones they are. Your students may find others; creative interpretation of the clues will allow possibilities we hadn't dreamed of.

Problems with more than one solution are important because they are like many problems in real life. Also:

- Some students believe there's always one answer in math. But math is richer and more flexible.

- Multiple solutions mean multiple routes to success. A less-experienced group may find one solution, and that may be an important achievement. A more-experienced group may find several. Very sophisticated students may explain how they know they have *all* solutions.

How do you deal with multiple solutions? Here are some ideas:

- Ask a probing question when a group finishes a problem: "Is this the only solution?"

- You may bring it up in debriefing. "Your group thinks Bengt weighs 125 pounds; let's hear what some other groups got..." and let the students discover they had different answers to the same problem.

Ultimately, you will develop a class culture in which students know that whenever they find one solution to a problem, they should look to see if there are others. (This is a good lesson in more than just math.)

Grade Level and Curriculum

These problems are designed to be appropriate for a problem-solving-oriented middle grades curriculum with high standards. Several exciting new curricula, generally based on multi-week units, are emerging in 1996 or have recently been published. Problems in this book will complement these curricula.

Many of the problems are also appropriate in high school. We do not mean that they are remedial (as you'll see when you look at them). Many of the curriculum issues are still relevant: we want high-school students to understand proportion, to deal effectively with data, to make scale drawings, and so forth. We also want to give them experience working in groups. High-school students have a bigger mathematical toolkit, so they will address these problems at a different level. For example, while an eighth-grade group may solve *Lillian's Island* (page 145) by setting up a proportion, students who know symbolic algebra can write and solve an equation.

See pages 190–191 for information on curricula available when this book was printed. For updates, come to our web site: http://www.eeps.com

Relaxing the Rules

It's strange not to show your clues to anyone in the group. In the classroom, most students eventually look at one another's cards. The rule is important, however, because it forces participation by all, and gives each person some ownership. It helps keep students from giving their clues away—and checking out.

You might relax the rule in two situations:

First, it may be important for some groups to start by working together on the individual clues—perhaps in partners—helping each other interpret them. Eventually, students learn to handle their clues alone.

Second, once students get good at working in groups—with their own clues—we can admit that the rule is artificial and rescind it. This is OK, and you can judge when to allow it. It's important that this be accompanied by true group collaboration. To reach this level of collaboration, it may help to engage students in frequent discussions of how to work in groups.

Page 26 has a letter to the students about this issue that you may use as you see fit.

Language

These materials depend heavily on reading and understanding English. Challenging problems can be especially difficult for students who are learning the language. Here are some ideas that may help:

- Provide primary language support by translating critical terms or even entire problems. We have translated only *Balloons* (page 78) and *Golden Arches* (page 23)—and only into Spanish.

- Create visual displays (with labels in English) that illustrate specific ideas.

- Consistently use the same terms for the same concept.

- Second-language learners may know certain words in a social context and not in an academic context. A good example is "mean." Clarify these words as appropriate.

- Choose some problems where the clues are largely visual, symbolic, or numeric. The *Points of View* problems (pages 102–105) are good examples.

The social environment and the mechanics of the lesson are equally critical:

- Model the mechanics of the group process. Before the first problem, bring a group (one that includes English language learners) to the front of the class and let the class watch as they open the envelope, pass out the clues, and begin to work on the problem. In this way, students may get a picture of what they're expected to do.

- An alternative scheme is to pass out clues to everyone. Then, as a whole class, discuss one clue at a time. Each student sees what it is like to figure out what an individual clue means, but no one is on the spot—in danger of slowing down the group.

- Debrief the modeling. We hope English-speaking students develop empathy and respect for second-language learners. Discuss what happened when various group members did not understand something. "How would you like people to help you so you can understand?" "How can they help so you can still do your own thinking?"

- During group work, let students work in pairs. For example, in a group of four, let two students work together with two clues so they can help each other understand the clues and the task.

- Encourage bilingual students who have become proficient in English to act as *language mediators*. These students help in two ways: they help second-language learners understand the English, and they help these students communicate good ideas to native English speakers in the group. That way, you get help, kids get help in the groups, and the language mediators learn a lot and earn respect from their peers.

- Monitor for understanding throughout the process.

Finally, when you find problems or strategies that work especially well, let us know. Your input can help us improve future publications.

Special thanks to Grace Dávila Coates and the EQUALS "Writers' Block" for help with this page.

If You Translate a Problem

Send it to us electronically (publications@eeps.com), and—if you give us permission—we'll post it on our web site.

You can find the postings at http://www.eeps.com

Individual Work

"When they work in groups, how do you know if they're learning?" Volumes have been written recently about assessment, especially "authentic" or "performance" assessment, rubrics, formal and informal observation, peer response groups—it goes on and on. And even if your students don't yet keep mathematics portfolios, you've heard about them. Some of these techniques work fine for groups: you can collect the scratch paper groups use, have group presentations, or ask students to turn in group papers. But individual work is important, too—and you can use the group setting to nurture an individual assignment.

Problems of the Week

One way is to let the group task segue into an individual task. Many of these problems—especially the ones with the keyword "POW" (Problem of the Week) at the bottom of the page—are rich enough that they naturally last longer than a single period and can elicit a written product from the students. (Of course, other problems may be suitable as well, depending on your students' ages and experience. A quick exercise for an eighth grader might be worth a lot of attention from a ten-year-old in fifth grade.)

When the problem itself demands written work, you have a choice: you can let the group do it or change the instruction to make it an individual assignment. Some teachers use "hard" group problems as POWs. On Monday, groups meet and get the clue cards. The point is not to *solve* the problem, but simply to understand what the problem is and to begin to work. Then the whole page is posted or handed out, and individual solutions are due Friday.

This helps to ensure that more people understand the assignment, and gives students who need a little "down time" a chance to more fully understand the meaning of the parts of the problem.

There are countless variations. Maybe you have group POWs. Maybe there's another group session on Wednesday to work on the POW. Maybe the POW is an extension (from clue ○ or △) of a problem the group solves in class. Maybe it's a question students pose during the debriefing.

Writing

We in Mathematics have a great deal to learn from our colleagues in Language Arts. Programs such as the Writers' Workshop have revolutionized writing instruction. We can capitalize on—and complement—work in English by insisting that students write in math as well.

It may not go well at first. One Guindon cartoon caption reads, "Writing is Nature's way of telling you how sloppy your thinking is." But writing—even in as unfamiliar a setting as math class—gets better with practice. Here are three pieces of advice: First, writing need not be elaborate. It can even begin as a list (write down everything you can about percents). Second, not every paper is a publication. Don't sweat spelling, punctuation, or grammar unless it will be published (e.g., go into a portfolio). Finally, the real measure of quality writing is communication, so (even though you are their real audience) let students read aloud to one another or read one another's work, and comment on what they liked and where they had additional questions. *Then have them do another draft.*

The result? You'll have a rich and durable record of student thinking.

Problems and Strategies

Resource

Georg Pólya's *How To Solve It* (Doubleday, 1957), is the indispensable ancestor of many problem-solving books.

One of Pólya's suggestions is to solve a simpler problem first. For example, you might substitute easier numbers. Or if a problem is three-dimensional, you might solve it in two dimensions first.

A genuine problem is an encounter with a new and unexpected situation. If you know what to do already—for example, if you've seen the teacher solve one just like it with different numbers—it's an exercise. Exercises are good for you, but you need problems in your diet as well.

How do you learn to be a good problem solver? By solving problems: there's no substitute for experience. And though grinding through problem after problem will help, it will help even more if you think about the *strategies* you use to solve problems. A teacher can help students recognize and use effective problem solving strategies—*without* telling them what to do.

As a teacher watching groups solve problems, you will see students using new strategies on their own. You can point them out to the students in discussion so they don't get lost. ("Tammy, I saw your group making an unusual kind of chart. Would one of you explain to the class what it is and how it helped you solve the problem?") Some teachers keep a piece of butcher paper on the wall. Students add new strategies to the list as they discover them; then they can refer to their own list when they get stuck. You can seed the list with a couple of the most famous strategies, such as guess and check, work backwards, and make it simpler. We'll discuss some especially important strategies in this section.

Use Manipulatives

Some older students think blocks and beans are just for little kids. Wrong! Even as formal, abstract, and analytical adults, concrete tools can help us make sense of a new and unexpected situation.

For example, if a problem has someone going from point A to point B, it helps to have a block represent the someone and to draw Point A and Point B. Physically moving the block makes the situation more concrete. And, of course, if you're supposed to draw a structure specified in the clues, there's no substitute for building it first.

But manipulatives are good for more than just spatial problems. You can make labels for names and use beans to represent values. A pile of twelve beans on the "Tom" label means he's twelve years old. The person with the clue that Tom is twice as old as Letty will watch Letty's label and make sure that she has six beans. By moving the beans around, you can easily change the values of these variables. You'll be doing algebra without ever using your eraser.

Manipulatives also help communication among group members by making thinking visible.

Guess, Check, Analysis, and Algebra

Some people think you're supposed to grow out of "guess and check." Not so—as long as you remember the "…and check" part. Trying things out *and checking the results* gives you a feel for a situation. If you record your guesses and checks in a table, draw them in diagrams, and graph them, you're not being haphazard—you're being a mathematician. Such guesses are the foundation of being analytical and are a necessary adjunct to using symbolic algebra.

Draw a Picture

It's amazing how many people will try to solve *Ned & Kristin* (page 25) without drawing a picture. If you have to visualize the problem situation in order to tell whether to add or subtract the numbers, by all means draw it. It will act as a check on your mind's eye and may reveal more information than you thought.

Pictures come in many forms, including:

- **Maps**. A map shows the relationship between things in space. Often, when you translate the clues in a "Directions" problem into a map, you immediately see what you need to know. And if you don't make a map, you're doomed.

- **Diagrams**. Diagrams are stylized pictures. They show the essential parts of a situation and how they're related. Other diagrams show the *logical* relationship among parts of the problem. Networks (or *graphs*, in the discrete-math sense) show how things are connected or how they depend on one another. A family tree is an example of this kind of diagram.

- **Scale Drawings**. Though not all drawings require this much sophistication, scale drawings often show you a solution that you need trigonometry or the Pythagorean Theorem to figure out otherwise. By the time a mathematically powerful student finishes eighth grade, he or she should be able to decide whether a scale drawing would be useful, create one if it is (for a fairly simple situation), and draw correct conclusions from it.

Make a Table

Sometimes, the real problem is organizing information. A simple table can make all the difference. Students need practice creating tables in different contexts: timetables for schedules, t-tables for functions, tables to record guesses and checks. And, of course, the columns may need to be labeled.

When you organize data or guesses, a pattern may emerge. You need this skill to go on to using functions and symbolic representations.

Make a Graph

Once the data are organized, the next step may be to make them visual with a graph. What graph depends on the problem. Maybe it calls for a point plot, or a pie chart, or a column graph. Maybe it calls for box-and-whisker or stem-and-leaf or a scatterplot. But the right graph can be the cornerstone of a convincing argument.

Make a Ratio or Proportion

Many of the problems in this book have to do with ratio and proportion. You may be able to solve them using algebra or trigonometry, but you don't have to. Instead, you can guess and check—and then set up a ratio with the result.

Make the Next Draft

Sometimes, all we teachers see is scratch paper and first drafts. Taking the work into the next draft—neatening it up, eliminating some wrong turns, and so forth—can help students' understanding and greatly improve the communication in the problem solution.

The Teacher's Role

Sometimes parents—and some teachers—worry that group work means that the gifted kids are teaching the class instead of the teacher. If you explain that you're acting as a facilitator, it sounds like so much educational gobbledygook. It doesn't help that acting as a good facilitator is hard work. It goes against the grain of what we were taught a teacher should be: a dispenser of information. And, frankly, a lot of us (the author included) love to dispense. Especially when we're right.

Yet when we facilitate instead of dispense, kids learn better. It's like the "teach me to fish and you feed me for a lifetime" saying. The problem is, we're in the habit of passing out dead fish. That's what everybody expects.

Breaking the Omniscience Habit

It takes a while for a class to get used to depending on one another instead of on you. It's easier for them if you tell them when they're right and wrong, and if you explain things to them every time they don't understand. If you ask them to figure it out for themselves, you're giving them a new responsibility. They may rebel. You can help by being unrelentingly encouraging—without giving in.

The extra time you get because they're working in groups is not free time. Use every second to learn about your students. As a facilitator, you still direct the class and determine what happens next. Here are some observations that might help you describe the process to a skeptical parent (or a skeptical self):

- Being a facilitator means choosing long-term goals over short-term goals. You may be disappointed in the short-term *appearance* of learning, but in groups, what gets learned is more likely to stay learned.

- Direct instruction has a place, but "telling" the class should be a deliberate choice (some even say a last resort) rather than a reflex.

- When you don't tell students whether their answer is right, that doesn't mean you don't *care* whether the answer is right. When they have to convince you, you show them you value self-reliance and sound thinking.

- If you *intervene*, for example, to praise an individual, to take care of a disruption, or to tell a group that they're on the wrong track, you're taking power away from the group and making them rely on you. If you *interact* with the group, by asking them what they think, by asking how they will take care of the disruption, by asking them where they think this line of reasoning is going, you help them take responsibility. Ask, don't tell.

- The less you say, the more you can hear. And the more you hear, the more you'll know about what your students need.

- The most talented student has needs. We often think of "talent" in math as purely computational or analytical. Social skills are just as important.

- There are plenty of situations in school where there is one right answer and where speed and memory count the most. Time spent in group work doesn't replace all that, but instead gives students a broader range of experience.

Answers

Not giving answers is hard. Students need feedback, but see if they can get the answers from their group and from the class. Students will ask if they got it right. Respond with a question: "What do you think?" "Does anyone have any doubts?" "How did you check your work?" You might also state facts and ask for clarification: "I see you made a drawing and a table of values." "I see you made labels. What do the beans represent?"

But shouldn't the *teacher* know the answers? Teachers don't have time to do all the problems.

True. But while you don't have to do every problem, you should *read* any problem you give out, and you should have done enough problems—preferably with a group of your colleagues—to know what it's like.

Even so, one teacher we talked to was unsatisfied until we brainstormed this solution: Have the students compile a class answer book. When students write up their best answers to a problem, they are in charge. And a student book does not have the dangerous, disembodied authority of some distant publisher. If next year's students come up with a better answer, so be it.

Some teachers praise the lack of answers in this book. One said, "I'm so glad the book has no answers. When the kids say, 'Mrs. K., what *is* the right answer?' I can honestly say, 'I don't know. But can you convince me yours is right?'"

Another teacher said, "If I knew the answer, I would stop them as soon as they found it. As it is, they have to keep going. They keep working on the problem until they're convinced. And then I know they understand."

The right answer is still important, but notice how these teachers emphasize convincing argument and understanding. Even if you don't know the answer, you can tell if a group's reasoning is sound.

Web Answer Collection

If you don't want to make a class answer book, or you just want to be part of a larger, answer-seeking community, here's a high-tech offer: As of summer, 1997, we're collecting *student* solutions to problems and posting them on the worldwide web. If you go to our web site and don't find an answer, that means that no student has sent one in. This is your chance for fame and glory: submit one and we'll post it. As you know, we're interested in the process as well as the final product. So tell us how you did it. And, while we may comment on solutions, we will not guarantee that the answers we post will be correct.

Visit **http://www.eeps.com/united.html** and follow links from there to the answers. To submit an answer, send it by email (and you can attach a file in most formats) to **answers@eeps.com**.

What if your solution is different from the one on the web? What if you got the same answer but in a different way? By all means send it in. Our postings will be limited only by our energy, your creativity, a little editorial prerogative, and, of course, disk space.

Trouble in Paradise

Group work is not a panacea. It can help students enjoy mathematics and make it their own. It can help students who never used to participate find new confidence and power. Unfortunately, sometimes it seems to have the opposite effect: some students rebel, withdraw, or become more befuddled than before. Someone might say, "it's no worse than it used to be," but that isn't very helpful.

Sometimes, even when the class knows how to work together, a problem will bomb. The class just doesn't get the math—even when you thought they should know it. One possibility is that the students do not in fact have some skill you thought they had. Another possibility is that they have the skill, but not securely enough to use it in an unusual situation. For example, they may be able to add fractions in exercises, but not when the addition is in some context. In either case, you can treat the bombed problem as a message that tells you what the class needs. You may decide to let it pass for now, you may decide to give them another problem, or you may decide to try some direct instruction.

The Problems Are Hard

It's different, however, when you look at the problems and they just seem too hard for your kids.

It's true that many of these problems *are* hard, especially for younger students. They have been written so that students who are experienced enough to use proportion (for example) flexibly in problem solving can demonstrate a high standard of performance. Many (especially the ones marked "POW" or "Challenging") also demand that students spend considerable time and thought on them.

These problems have been field-tested by real live children of mixed ability in many different classrooms. Many of the students were experienced at problem solving and group work. For them, some problems were exercises, some were just right, some were hard, some were too hard. That's what we want to see. On the other hand, students for whom these were their first group experience had a very hard time. Their problem was not the math, but marshaling the group's resources to solve the problem.

Give yourself and your students a break. After all, this is not a contest to see who cooperates the best. If your students are completely lost with some of the problems, pose different problems and encourage persistence. You may find—as many teachers do—that your students can actually do more of the math than you thought.

An Equity Problem

What if some students are giving up and letting others do all the work? When you look more closely, you may see that some students really don't understand what their own clues mean, and therefore can't contribute effectively. Furthermore, you may see that the nonparticipants are English language learners, or children of color, or girls, or members of some other group that is not well-represented in mathematical fields. It looks as if you're making equity problems worse instead of better.

Here are some ideas:

- Try giving students some time to think about their clues *before* they start talking.

- Let students work in pairs.

- Set up an "advisory table" with a teacher or older student.

- Define unfamiliar terms ahead of time.

- Use techniques for second-language learners—even if the students are native English speakers (See page 14).

- Try a jigsaw (see below).

One Strategy: Jigsaw

You can adapt the "jigsaw" technique to give students a chance to learn about their own clues before they have to use them in the group.

- Arrange students so that they are sitting with others who have the *same* clue.

- First, each student writes individually about what they know from their own clue.

- Next, these "same-clue" groups discuss what the clue means. The individuals add to what they've written.

- Finally, students take their notes back to the regular groups. They've thought about their own clues quite a bit by now, so they'll participate more effectively.

Not all problems work this way. Before you use a problem as a jigsaw, think about what you can know from an individual clue. If it's a "data" problem like *East and West* (page 88) it's quite clear. The problems in *Pyramid Schemes*, however (pages 128–135) are inappropriate for Jigsaw.

Jigsaw Logistics

One way to make the logistics work is to pass out the clues to your normal groups. Then bring the same-clue groups together. (You can identify same clues by the blip—▶, ▲, etc.—on the clues.) When the students have finished working in these same-clue groups, they return to their original groups to solve the problem.

Alternatively, you can use color to identify the sets. Then sort problems into same-clue sets (e.g., eight clues with ▲—but in different colors) before you pass them out to groups. After students write and discuss in these first groups, they then move to same-color groups ("all the greens get together…") to solve the problems. In this technique, students have to change groups only once, but you have to figure out the numbers more carefully ahead of time.

Creating New Problems

You may want more problems, or different ones. You can make more of your own, or, better yet, have your students make some. A blank problem is on page 184.

To invent a problem like these, you need an appropriate problem—one that is amenable to group solution. Once you have a good problem, you need to make up good clues, that is, clues that genuinely contribute without giving the whole thing away. Then make sure that the problem is solvable with the right number of clues.

Modify a problem

This can be as simple as changing the names of the kids, or changing the numbers to make the calculation different. Be careful, though; sometimes you can "break" a problem inadvertently by changing the numbers. It's awkward (but perhaps a teachable moment) when you've given students a problem where Elise turns out to be negative four years old or six meters tall.

Translate a problem

Another way to create a new problem is to translate one into another language. If you cannot, have students help. Translated clues will help students who know that language better than English—or make monolingual English students more understanding. (See opposite.)

Add a problem to a cluster

You can also find a cluster of problems you like in this book and make up new problems, based on the ones we have provided. You might make the new problem easier, or harder, or more focused on a particular concept. For example, if you're interested in box plots and stem-and-leaf, *Many Faces* (pages 85–88) has two problems that are relevant. Maybe you want one more like *East & West*, so you get some data from the Census appendix (page 186) and make a new problem.

Or maybe your students will be studying the area of a triangle, so you look at *Polygons*. Suppose the problems there aren't right for you. You might decide to make up three new problems: one about making a rectangle from a cut-up triangle, one about making a triangle from a cut-up rectangle, and one about measuring the base and height correctly and applying the formula.

Arcos Dorados®

Basado en la información de su grupo, ¿cree ud. que algún día habrá tantos restaurantes "McDonald's" en otros países como hay en los Estados Unidos? Si ud. cree que sí, ¿en qué año?

Restaurantes "McDonald's" en los EEUU:

año	#
1985	6972
1986	7272
1987	7567
1988	7907
1989	8270

Arcos Dorados®

¿Habrá algún día tantos restaurantes "McDonald's" en otros países como hay en los Estados Unidos?

Usted y su grupo deben ponerse de acuerdo acerca de la respuesta que encuentren, presentar un argumento convincente, y preparar una gráfica o cuadro que apoye dicho argumento.

Restaurantes "McDonald's" afuera de los EEUU:

año	#
1985	1929
1986	2138
1987	2344
1988	2606
1989	2892

Arcos Dorados®

¿Habrá algún día tantos restaurantes "McDonald's" en otros países como hay en los Estados Unidos? ¿Cuándo?

Ayúdele a su grupo a crear un cartel que apoye en forma convincente su respuesta. Una tabla, un cuadro o una gráfica podrían ayudar.

Restaurantes "McDonald's" en los EEUU:

año	#
1990	8576
1991	8764
1992	8959
1993	9283
1994	9744

Arcos Dorados®

¿Cuándo (si es que llega el día) cree ud. que llegará el día en que el número de restaurantes "McDonald's" afuera de los Estados Unidos será el mismo que el número de dichos restaurantes en los Estados Unidos? Ayúdele a su grupo a decidir. Cuando hayan decidido hagan un cartel que sirva de apoyo para su argumento.

Restaurantes "McDonald's" afuera de los EEUU:

año	#
1990	3227
1991	3654
1992	4134
1993	4710
1994	5461

Arcos Dorados®

Extensión: in 1994, el McDonald's promedio que había llevado por lo menos un año de estar abierto tenía $1,800,000 en ventas. ¡Guau!

Trabaje con su grupo, usando esa cifra para estimar el número de hamburguesas vendidas bajo les "Arcos Dorados" mundialmente in 1994. Tendrá que hacer algunas suposiciones.

Arcos Dorados®

Pista: se puede acercarse a este problema mirando la *diferencia* entre los números de restaurantes adentro y afuera de los EEUU; también se puede mirar la *proporción* de los números. ¿Cuál tiene el mejor sentido?

Fuente: *McDonald's Corporation 1994 Annual Report*. Usado con permiso.

from *United We Solve*

(English version on page 57)
Extrapolation, functions, graphing, range of answers. Group display. Cluster: Can You Relate?

Invent a New Cluster

Chances are a new cluster will be inspired either by context or by content. Here are some ideas and warnings:

- Look at an existing cluster and think about what constrains it. Then change the constraint. For example, *Arrange the Blocks* uses only cubes. What if you used pattern blocks? It might be two-dimensional, but you'd get different geometrical terms and different thinking.

- Think about different forms, for example, what if there were more than four clues. We have heard of teachers who invented problems where each student in the class had his or her own essential clue. Or what if students had to get up and measure something? There's no law that says they have to stay at tables.

- Remember what the problem is about. It's easy to forget the essence of the content, to make it so that the group only has to recognize a number pattern (say) instead of understand the situation.

- At first, be sure to test a new problem (with a small group if you can) before you use it with a class.

- Don't worry if your new problem doesn't work. Lots of ours never see print.

For example, suppose you're doing the unit *Dry and Wet Numbers* from Mathematics in Context (one of the new middle-grades curricula; it's published by Britannica). It's about positive and negative numbers, and has a framing context of boats in locks going up and down. Taking off from that, we designed the problem *Ned & Kristin* on page 25. What if each group designed a similar problem?

What Makes Rich Problems?

If we only knew! Sometimes a problem is rich enough that everyone can participate and no one can do it alone. Such a problem is hard to find, and it may not work in a different classroom. But a rich problem probably has several of the following attributes:

It's worth spending some time. When you do it, you naturally have to make or write something. And it's possible to explain your thinking, so you can write *how* you did it.

It's hard but not too hard. You should not immediately see to the end of the problem when you read it. You may even feel discouraged partway through. But working with a group and talking with others about it gets you over a stuck place.

You can look at it different ways. Maybe you can solve it with an equation, or a network, or a table, or by making a list, or by moving beans around.

It may be as much about organizing information as it is about the math topic. Maybe there's a diagram that looks like spaghetti until you figure out how to draw it, or a collection of numbers that have to be put into rows just so before you can describe the pattern.

▲ Ned & Kristin

Kristin is standing on a stool 42 cm high.

Ned is Kristin's pet spider.

How high is Ned now *compared to the top of the table*? Work with your group to figure it out.

▼ Ned & Kristin

Kristin's stool has three legs.

Ned was sitting on Kristin's hand, but then he jumped off and let out a strand of silk 108 cm long.

How high is Ned now *compared to the top of the table*?

◄ Ned & Kristin

The stool is next to a table whose top is 73 cm above the floor. Kristin is 159 cm tall.

How high is Ned now *compared to the top of the table*? Work with your group to figure it out.

► Ned & Kristin

Kristin's hand is held out at shoulder height, which, for Kristin, would be 135 cm if she were standing on the floor. But she is not standing on the floor.

How high is Ned *compared to the top of the table*? Work with your group to figure it out.

○ Ned & Kristin

Hint: Making a diagram will help with this problem.

Some of the information in this problem is not important.

How high is Ned now *compared to the top of the table*?

△ Ned & Kristin

From Kristin's shoulder to the top of her head is 24 cm.

How high is Ned now *compared to the top of the table*? Work with your group to figure it out.

Integers.

Cluster: none

Notes for Group Members

You will be working as a member of a group. Your group will have to solve a problem or complete a task, working together. You will get a clue of your own that has information on it. The group needs that information in order to do its work.

There's a rule, though, that says you can't *show* your clue to others. You may tell them about it. You may read it aloud. But you can't show them.

Why such a weird rule?

In the real world, you can see only a part of a big problem. Other people see different parts. You have different views, different perspectives, and you know different things. To solve the whole problem, you need to communicate:

- you have to tell others what you know;

- you have to listen to what they know;

- you have to take their ideas into account; and

- you have to make sure your ideas don't get lost.

Even so, we have to admit: keeping the clues hidden is a *gimmick*. It's a trick to get group members to talk together and work together. As you get better at working as a group, your teacher may relax that rule and let you see one another's cards. You will still have different perspectives. You will still need to communicate. You will still have to make sure the group's solution takes your own information into account.

You need to learn to do many things on your own, but we think working together is important too—especially on large problems. Something small you can do alone. Something big, you often need help—not just because there's a lot to do, but because you need different people's ideas.

One more thing: If you're used to working alone in mathematics, you may find it hard to work together. You may feel slow—that you're holding the group back. Or you may feel fast—that they're holding you back. Instead, think about this: working together is not about fast or slow. It's about how well everyone understands. And it's about everyone in the group doing his or her best work. Sometimes it takes a while to learn to work together, but it's worth it.

Patterns

Patterns are part of the mathematics curriculum beginning in preschool. Kindergarteners recognize, extend, and create simple patterns such as "circle, circle, square, circle, circle, square…". Patterns are more than simple sequences. Patterns can be two-dimensional, for example, a tessellation. Patterns can reflect causation or logic (such as the realization that whenever you multiply a whole number by two, you get an even number). Patterns don't even have to be deterministic (such as the discovery that seven comes up more than any other number when you roll two dice and add).

In middle school, students generalize patterns and use those patterns to figure out other things. The study of number sequences becomes the study of functions. The study of spatial patterns leads to conjecture and proof in geometry. And the study of patterns in real-life phenomena is part of science, statistics, and the study of systems.

The six clusters of problems in this broad category explore different aspects of generalizing from patterns. Of course, other problems in this book also have to do with patterns; these things can't easily be kept apart. But here, the pattern is the main thing.

Alien Number Systems

Materials: scratch paper, pencils, manipulatives

Math: number systems, number theory, place value

In each problem, the group has to figure out an "alien" number system or discover some of its properties. Some of these systems are "regular," that is, based on a place-value system, though different from our own. Others are more unusual, based on operations or repeated words or symbols. (Roman numerals fit into this category.)

Znorlian

This is a natural starter, accessible to fifth grade, and relatively straightforward.

- What is the biggest number you can write in Znorlian using the symbols that we know?

Geap

There are really two parts to this task: figuring out the values of the digits, and figuring out the smallest number that cannot be represented.

- How do you know that you can make every number less than (whatever they say)?

Spakk'r

Each clue has some Spakk'r first graders counting, but you don't know where they started. Can you infer the number system from the patterns in the number words?

- Do you have any other evidence to support your idea?

Diphland

Each Diphland number has two parts: a head and a tail, separated by a colon. The value of the number is the first minus the second. There are restrictions about which digits can be used. Each clue has a different question; three of the four are about divisibility rules in this system.

Lorith

This problem is about place value, but there is a different base in every place. When people do the others first, they will have a much easier time.

There are two tasks here: to figure out the number system, and then to practice it by making an eight-by-eight multiplication table. For some students, doing the times table is the reward for figuring it out; it doesn't require insight, just care and practice. If the times-table becomes busywork, you can cut it short.

- Explain how you constructed this number.

Roman Code

Now for the most alien system of all: Roman numerals.

What if there were Roman spies, and they wrote Roman numerals in code? We think there might be more than one solution to this, but we haven't found it. The optional clues remind students about Roman numerals. Do not use this problem if students have never seen that system.

Znorlian

In Znorlian, $\wedge$ means "one."

In Znorlian, the order of digits doesn't matter, so

$$\wedge \bowtie = \bowtie \wedge \quad \text{(Which is five.)}$$

What is the shortest way to write 21 in Znorlian?

Znorlian

Adding numbers in Znorlian is easy. Just put them together. For example,

$$\wedge \wedge = \triangledown$$

is an addition sentence adding $\wedge$ and $\wedge$.

What is the shortest way to write 21 in Znorlian?

Znorlian

In Znorlian, there are different ways to write some numbers. For example:

$$\bowtie \bowtie = \blacksquare = \triangledown \triangledown \triangledown \triangledown$$

What is the shortest way to write 21 in Znorlian?

Znorlian

Znorlians write subtraction using a minus sign, just as we do. (Their equals sign is the same, too.) In Znorlian,

$$\boxtimes - \triangledown = \triangledown \blacksquare \bowtie$$

What is the shortest way to write 21 in Znorlian?

Znorlian

Here are three ways to write "seven" in Znorlian:

$$\triangledown \wedge \triangledown \; \triangledown = \triangledown \bowtie \wedge = \bowtie \triangledown \wedge$$

What is the shortest way to write 21 in Znorlian?

Znorlian

With the first five digits in the Znorlian number system (not in order):

$$\triangledown \quad \bowtie \quad \boxtimes \quad \blacksquare \quad \wedge$$

You can write every number from 1 to 31 without using any double Znorlian digits.

What is the shortest way to write 21 in Znorlian?

from *United We Solve*

Number systems, multiple representations. Starter.

Cluster: Alien Number Systems

⋀ Geap!

On Geap, the digits they use for numbers are **G**, **E**, **A**, and **P**. To make a number, just put the digits together.

So since **A** = 5, **AA** = 10.

What's the smallest counting number that you *cannot* represent on Geap?

▼ Geap!

On Geap, as in Znorlian, order of the digits doesn't matter, so

$$\mathbf{Ep} = \mathbf{pE}$$

Both of these mean "24" on Geap.

What's the smallest counting number that you *cannot* represent on Geap?

◄ Geap!

On Geap, upper-case digits are positive, while lower-case are negative.

So **PA** = 6, but **pA** = 4.

Similarly, **pa** = –6, and **Pa** = –4.

What's the smallest counting number that you *cannot* represent on Geap?

► Geap!

On Geap, you may not use the same letter (upper- or lower-case) more than twice in a number. So while **GAA** (which means 135) is a number, **GaAA** is not.

What's the smallest counting number that you *cannot* represent on Geap?

○ Geap!

On Geap, numbers that are close to each other sometimes look different. For example, **AAPP** (12) is one less than **Eaapp** (13)

What's the smallest counting number that you cannot represent on Geap?

(The counting numbers are 1, 2, 3, and so forth. Not zero. Not negative. No fractions.)

△ Geap!

You can even make a few words! For example:

PEG = 151, or **Peg** = –149.

What's the smallest counting number that you cannot represent on Geap?

Extension: how many different ways can you represent zero on Geap?

from *United We Solve*

Number systems, negative numbers.

Cluster: Alien Number Systems

▲ Spakk'r

A class of Spakk'r first graders is counting:

"...babato, bababato, toto, batoto, babatoto, ..."

Too bad you don't know where they started.

How would you say 50 in Spakk'r?

▼ Spakk'r

A class of Spakk'r first graders is counting:

"...batoto, babatoto, bababatoto, tototo, batototo..."

Too bad you don't know where they started.

What does **batotoku** mean?

◄ Spakk'r

A class of Spakk'r first graders is counting:

"...babababatototo, ku, baku, babaku, bababaku, toku, ..."

Too bad you don't know where they started.

What does **babato** mean?

► Spakk'r

You hear class of Spakk'r first graders counting:

"...toku, batoku, babatoku, bababatoku, totoku,..."

But you don't know where they started.

How would you say "1" in Spakk'r?

○ Spakk'r

You come across a class of Spakk'r first graders. They're practicing counting. As you watch them, some are counting on their fingers. They have only four fingers on each hand.

How do you count in Spakk'r?

△ Spakk'r

A class of Spakk'r first graders is counting. You hear:

"...babababatototokukuku, pa, bapa, babapa, bababapa, ..."

But you don't know where they started.

How do you count in Spakk'r?

---

from *United We Solve*

Number systems, counting, number bases, multiple questions. **Cluster: Alien Number Systems**

▲ Lorith

In Lorith, they write numbers with digits like ours, but the "places" are different. Only the "ones" place is the same.

So while **1** (in Lorith) = 1 (for us), **111** (Lorith) = 9 (us).

Your job, as a group, is to make a Lorithian multiplication table up to 110 by 110.

▼ Lorith

In Lorith, the third digit from the end is the "sixes." That means that

100 (in Lorith) = 6 (for us).

Your job, as a group, is to make a Lorithian multiplication table up to **110** by **110**.

◄ Lorith

In Lorith, the only digits that can appear in the last place are **0** and **1**. In the next-to-last, **0, 1**, and **2** are OK.

That means that **12** is not a number for the Lorithians, while **21** is. (It means five.)

Your job, as a group, is to make a Lorithian multiplication table up to **110** by **110**.

► Lorith

You need four digits in Lorith to represent any number larger than 23. For example,

2010 (in Lorith) = 50 (for us)

Your job, as a group, is to make a Lorithian multiplication table up to **110** by **110** (don't worry—that's only eight by eight).

○ Lorith

Lorithian mathematicians have long known that multiples of three always end in **00** (as in **200**, which is 12) or **11** (as in **311**, which is 21).

Extension: You can use this fact to check your multiplication table, but can you and your group explain why this is true?

△ Lorith

Here are some Lorithian addition facts:

$$21 + 21 = 120$$
$$100 + 100 = 200$$
$$101 + 101 = 210$$
$$110 + 110 = 220$$

Use them to help your group make (or check) a Lorithian multiplication table up to **110** by **110**.

from *United We Solve*

Number systems, place value. Group display.

Cluster: Alien Number Systems

Diphland

All numbers in Diphland consist of two parts, separated by a colon. They call the first part the head, and the last the tail. In Diphland, the head can never have fewer digits than the tail, so 9:22 is not a number.

What's the easiest way to tell if a Diphland number is even?

Diphland

The head of a Diphland number uses only the digits 3, 6, and 9. So 33:26 (which means 7) is a number, whereas 26:33 is not.

Minh thinks it's impossible to represent the number 6 in Diphland. Can you make a convincing argument one way or the other?

Diphland

There is often more than one way to represent a number in Diphland, for example, "one" could be 3:2 or 9:8 or even 663:662.

You and your group have four things to do to finish this problem. They're described on four different cards.

Diphland

The value of a number in Diphland is the value of the head minus the value of the tail. You figure out those values just as you do normal numbers.

What's the easiest way to tell if a Diphland number is a multiple of three?

Diphland

The tail of a Diphland number uses only the digits 2, 4, 6, and 8. So 93:62 (which means 31) is a number, while 62:93 is not.

In Diphland, how can you tell whether a number is divisible by 10? Do you think you can make all the numbers that are divisible by 10?

Diphland

Remember that the digits 0, 5, and 7 can never appear in Diphland numbers.

Hint: It might help to make a systematic list of some numbers you can make.

from *United We Solve*

Number systems, divisibility tests, multiple questions.

Cluster: Alien Number Systems

Roman Code

The following is in Roman numerals. But it's in code. Each letter stands for one of the "Roman digits" I, V, X, L, or C.

$$ET + T = EA$$

Work with your group to crack this code.

Roman Code

The following is in Roman numerals. But it's in code. Each letter stands for one of the "Roman digits" I, V, X, L, or C.

$$AR + A = R$$

Work with your group to crack this code.

Roman Code

The following is in Roman numerals. But it's in code. Each letter stands for one of the "Roman digits" I, V, X, L, or C.

$$RS - T = ARTS$$

Work with your group to crack this code.

Roman Code

The following is in Roman numerals. But it's in code. Each letter stands for one of the "Roman digits" I, V, X, L, or C.

$$TS \times A = EA$$

Work with your group to crack this code.

Roman Code

In Roman numerals, if an I or an X precedes a larger number, it's subtracted. So

IX = 9, XL = 40, XLIX = 49, XC = 90, XCIX = 99, and so forth.

You never subtract a V or L. You might think that "VC" would be 95. Nope. It's XCV.

Roman Code

The basics in Rome:

I = 1, V = 5, X = 10, L = 50, and C = 100.

In Roman numerals, the big numbers have to come first unless there is a subtraction, so CLXXII = 172. You'd never write it "LIICXX."

from *United We Solve*

copyright © 1996 by eeps media

Number systems, codes, Roman numerals.

Cluster: Alien Number Systems

Mystery Operations

Materials: none, but see note below

Math: number, operations, generalizing from patterns

Note: The instructions for these problems ask students not to write anything down and not to use manipulatives. They are not to show their clues, but only talk and listen; they may find themselves listening more carefully than they usually do. If you don't like that, you can simply tell the students to ignore that instruction! In that case, provide manipulatives, paper, and pencil.

By the time you get to #4, you may want to let them write. #5 is quite hard and obscure, so you may want to save it for students who need something especially challenging. Beyond #3, problems are appropriate only in grade 7 or later.

These are kind of like "function machine" problems, but, since the operations are binary, they require two inputs.

An important issue is how the group comes to express their generalization of the operation. Sophisticated, older students may use eqations or formulas, but they aren't necessary. Learning how to express these kinds of mathematical relationships in many ways is an important part of mathematical communication.

General Questions

Interesting debriefing questions include:

- What was it like not to write anything? How did you remember what other people said in order to check your group's idea?

- How did you and your group "say" the operation? What words did you use when you were reading your clues?

- Does the commutative property hold for this operation? How do you know?

- The problem asks you to "figure out" the operation. What does it mean to figure it out?

Mystery Op 1

This is relatively easy; experienced kids get theories about the operation just from their own clues. The operation is based on addition.

Mystery Op 2

This is a little tougher. The operation is based on multiplication, with a little subtraction thrown in. Note that the associative property does not hold for this operation (see clues ▲ and ▼).

Mystery Op 3

Some people see this one right away; others ponder over it for some time. This operation is also not associative. And in clue ◯, Enoch is wrong. Probably too hard for most fifth graders.

Mystery Op 4

This one is fun, probably starting in about seventh grade. The operation is not commutative. If they're stuck, you might ask "How do you get these numbers with regular operations? Do you see any special numbers you recognize on your clues?" (Clues ▼, ◀, and ▶ have operations that result in perfect squares: 25, 36, and 49).

Mystery Op 5

This is included as a challenge for the talented, persistent, and experienced. You may have thought about this operation before, but probably not with fractions.

▲ Mystery Op 1

Your group's job is to figure out the mystery operation, ✳. But there's a special rule: You may only talk in this problem. No writing. No manipulatives.

Here is your clue:

$$2 ✳ 3 = 7 .$$

▼ Mystery Op 1

Your group's job is to figure out the mystery operation, ✳. But there's a special rule: You may only talk in this problem. No writing. No manipulatives.

Here is your clue:

$$3 ✳ 3 ✳ 4 = 14 .$$

◄ Mystery Op 1

Your group's job is to figure out the mystery operation, ✳. But there's a special rule: You may only talk in this problem. No writing. No manipulatives.

Here is your clue:

$$8 ✳ 8 = 18 .$$

► Mystery Op 1

Your group's job is to figure out the mystery operation, ✳. But there's a special rule: You may only talk in this problem. No writing. No manipulatives.

Here is your clue:

$$1 ✳ 6 = 9 .$$

○ Mystery Op 1

Your group's job is to figure out the mystery operation, ✳. But there's a special rule: You may only talk in this problem. No writing. No manipulatives.

Here is your clue:

$$1 ✳ 1 = 4 .$$

△ Mystery Op 1

Your group's job is to figure out the mystery operation, ✳. But there's a special rule: You may only talk in this problem. No writing. No manipulatives.

Here is your clue:

$$0 ✳ 4 = 6 .$$

from *United We Solve*

Operations, functions. Starter.

Cluster: Mystery Operations

▲ Mystery Op 2

Your group's job is to figure out the mystery operation, ❖. But there's a special rule: You may only talk in this problem. No writing. No manipulatives.

Here is your clue:

$$2 ❖ 3 = 5 \text{ and } 3 ❖ (3 ❖ 4) = 32$$

▼ Mystery Op 2

Your group's job is to figure out the mystery operation, ❖. But there's a special rule: You may only talk in this problem. No writing. No manipulatives.

Here is your clue:

$$(3 ❖ 3) ❖ 4 = 31 \text{ and } 2 ❖ 2 = 3$$

◄ Mystery Op 2

Your group's job is to figure out the mystery operation, ❖. But there's a special rule: You may only talk in this problem. No writing. No manipulatives.

Here is your clue:

$$5 ❖ 5 = 24 \text{ and } 1 ❖ 1 = 0$$

► Mystery Op 2

Your group's job is to figure out the mystery operation, ❖. But there's a special rule: You may only talk in this problem. No writing. No manipulatives.

Here is your clue:

$$4 ❖ 2 = 7 \text{ and } 3 ❖ 3 = 8$$

○ Mystery Op 2

Your group's job is to figure out the mystery operation, ❖. But there's a special rule: You may only talk in this problem. No writing. No manipulatives.

Here is your clue:

$$3 ❖ 4 = 11 .$$

△ Mystery Op 2

Your group's job is to figure out the mystery operation, ❖. But there's a special rule: You may only talk in this problem. No writing. No manipulatives.

Here is your clue:

$$0 ❖ 4 = -1 .$$

from *United We Solve*

Operations, functions, associative property.

Cluster: Mystery Operations

▲ Mystery Op 3

Your group's job is to figure out the mystery operation, ⊞. But there's a special rule: You may only talk in this problem. No writing. No manipulatives.

Here is your clue:

$$4 ⊞ 4 = 4$$

▼ Mystery Op 3

Your group's job is to figure out the mystery operation, ⊞. But there's a special rule: You may only talk in this problem. No writing. No manipulatives.

Here is your clue:

$$6 ⊞ 10 = 8.$$

◄ Mystery Op 3

Your group's job is to figure out the mystery operation, ⊞. But there's a special rule: You may only talk in this problem. No writing. No manipulatives.

Here is your clue:

$$(4 ⊞ 6) ⊞ 7 = 6.$$

► Mystery Op 3

Your group's job is to figure out the mystery operation, ⊞. But there's a special rule: You may only talk in this problem. No writing. No manipulatives.

Here is your clue:

$$3 ⊞ 7 = 5.$$

○ Mystery Op 3

Extension: Enoch looked at this problem and said, "I can make a generalization based on the clues. If a, b, and c are numbers so that

$$a ⊞ b = c,$$

then $c \leq b$."

Is Enoch right? Can you make a convincing argument why or why not?

△ Mystery Op 3

Your group's job is to figure out the mystery operation, ⊞.

A special clue, true for all values of a:

$$a ⊞ a = a.$$

Extension: Can you explain why it's always true?

from *United We Solve*

Operations, functions.

Cluster: Mystery Operations

▲ Mystery Op 4

Your group's job is to figure out the mystery operation, ✐. But there's a special rule: You may only talk in this problem. No writing. No manipulatives.

Here are your clues:

$$4 ✐ 4 = 15 \quad \text{and} \quad 2 ✐ 6 = 7.$$

▼ Mystery Op 4

Your group's job is to figure out the mystery operation, ✐. But there's a special rule: You may only talk in this problem. No writing. No manipulatives.

Here are your clues:

$$6 ✐ 2 = 15 \quad \text{and} \quad 8 ✐ 6 = 49.$$

◄ Mystery Op 4

Your group's job is to figure out the mystery operation, ✐. But there's a special rule: You may only talk in this problem. No writing. No manipulatives.

Here are your clues:

$$7 ✐ 2 = 18 \quad \text{and} \quad 6 ✐ 4 = 25.$$

► Mystery Op 4

Your group's job is to figure out the mystery operation, ✐. But there's a special rule: You may only talk in this problem. No writing. No manipulatives.

Here are your clues:

$$1 ✐ 1 = 0 \quad \text{and} \quad 7 ✐ 5 = 36.$$

○ Mystery Op 4

Your group's job is to figure out the mystery operation, ✐. But there's a special rule: You may only talk in this problem. No writing. No manipulatives.

A special clue, true for all values of a:

$$1 ✐ a = 0$$

△ Mystery Op 4

Your group's job is to figure out the mystery operation, ✐. But there's a special rule: You may only talk in this problem. No writing. No manipulatives.

A special clue, true for all values of a:

$$a ✐ 0 = a - 1$$

from *United We Solve*

Operations, functions, commutative property.

Cluster: Mystery Operations

▲ Mystery Op 5

Your group's job is to figure out the mystery operation, ▲.

Here are your clues:

$$6 \blacktriangle 8 = 24 \quad \text{and} \quad 1/3 \blacktriangle 1/2 = 1.$$

▼ Mystery Op 5

Your group's job is to figure out the mystery operation, ▲.

Here are your clues:

$$3 \blacktriangle 3 = 3 \quad \text{and} \quad 1 \blacktriangle 2/3 = 2.$$

◄ Mystery Op 5

Your group's job is to figure out the mystery operation, ▲.

Here are your clues:

$$7 \blacktriangle 5 = 35 \quad \text{and} \quad 3/4 \blacktriangle 1/6 = 3/2.$$

► Mystery Op 5

Your group's job is to figure out the mystery operation, ▲.

Here are your clues:

$$4 \blacktriangle 12 = 12 \quad \text{and} \quad 2 \blacktriangle 3/4 = 6.$$

○ Mystery Op 5

Your group's job is to figure out the mystery operation, ▲.

A special clue, true if $a > 1$:

$$1 \blacktriangle a > 1.$$

△ Mystery Op 5

Your group's job is to figure out the mystery operation, ▲.

A special clue, true for all values of a:

$$a \blacktriangle a = a$$

from *United We Solve*

Operations, functions. Challenging.

Cluster: Mystery Operations

Fractal Automata

Materials: special "brick-grid" mat (following each problem page), graph paper, colored pencils, markers, or crayons (alternatively, *lots* of colored cubes or bricks)

Math: discrete math, formal systems, recursion, cellular automata, fractals

This cluster is less about solving a problem than about following directions carefully and producing a group art project. We don't expect middle grade students to analyze cellular automata or fractals in earnest (or even to use those terms) but we can give them experiences that will help them understand the concepts—and to feel so comfortable with the mathematical guts that they don't get blown away by the vocabulary.

Each group member has one or more "coloring rules" to follow. All each person has to do is look for a pattern of bricks, and color the brick above it if they find it. As more bricks get colored in, more of their pattern appears, and gradually the big pattern emerges. In that way, this activity has some of the same satisfaction of knitting (if you like it) where a period of careful work without deep thought produces something ordered and wonderful.

The trick is to avoid coloring in the bricks you aren't responsible for. Consider asking students to check each other.

These are fragile activities in the sense that it's easy to make a single mistake that changes the eventual result. But as long as no one makes *consistent* mistakes, the sorts of patterns that emerge should be like those on a "correct" page. This is a wonderful property of chaotic systems. The flap of a butterfly's wings in China may indeed change the weather in New York, but the clouds that appear will inevitably look like clouds.

Some Questions

To follow up on the mathematics, *you* will have to ask questions of the groups. Here are some suggestions:

- What patterns do you see?

- How does your design compare with other groups'? What's the same? What's different?

- With this many colors (and this many bricks controlling the outcomes) how many rules are there altogether? How do you know?

- What would it have looked like if you put a red brick *here* in the bottom row?

- What would it have looked like if the bottom row started out all blue?

- Were there any rules you never used?

- What effect do the edge rules have?

Sierpinski Bricks

This is the classic. There are only four rules, and they make the amazing, self-similar Sierpinski Triangle. This is the same pattern you get when you color Pascal's Triangle one color for even and one for odd. So there are extensions: do the exercise for Pascal's Triangle and challenge the class to explain why the patterns are the same.

Another important extension is to let students invent their own coloring rules (start simple: two colors, four rules, one for each possible combination of two bricks) to see that the Sierpinski rules are special: most others make boring—or at least more predictable—patterns.

Brackets!

This has a different sort of pattern, more complex. There are still two colors, but each new block is determined by *three* blocks instead of two. To make rules for all combinations of three blocks means eight rules altogether, spread among the four cards. Since we're using three blocks, the underlying pattern is a grid rather than a staggered "brick" pattern. Use page 45 for the students to color.

We think this pattern repeats after 14 rows if you color the bottom row all yellow. But if you don't—for example, if you add two red blocks at the edge of the bottom row—you get a different effect. Let groups compare their patterns to others with slightly different starting conditions.

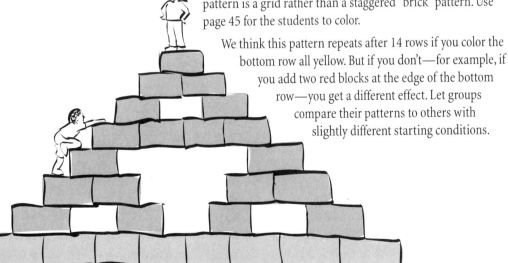

▲ Sierpinski Bricks

If you see a blue brick directly to the left of a yellow brick, color the brick above them *blue*.

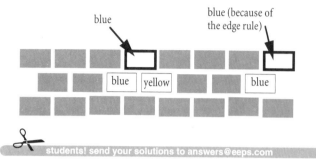

blue

blue (because of the edge rule)

blue   yellow

blue

▼ Sierpinski Bricks

If you see two blue bricks next to one another, color the brick above them *yellow*.

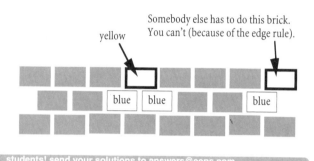

yellow

Somebody else has to do this brick. You can't (because of the edge rule).

blue   blue

blue

◄ Sierpinski Bricks

If you see a yellow brick directly to the left of a blue brick, color the brick above them *blue*.

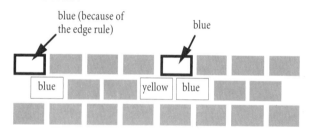

blue (because of the edge rule)

blue

blue   yellow   blue

► Sierpinski Bricks

If you see two yellow bricks next to one another, color the brick above them *yellow*.

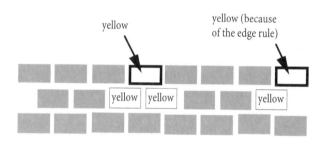

yellow

yellow (because of the edge rule)

yellow   yellow

yellow

❖ Sierpinski Bricks

Everybody should read this before you read your own clues.

In this activity, you're going to color in a brick wall according to certain rules. You will color a brick *blue* or *yellow* depending on the colors of the bricks below it. Your group can substitute any two contrasting colors as long as you agree. You'll need four crayons or markers—two of each color.

At the beginning, color the whole bottom row yellow except for one brick in the middle, which will be blue.

The edge rule: If a brick hangs over space because it's on the edge, *pretend that the space is colored yellow*. If this doesn't make sense yet, it will!

from *United We Solve*

Discrete math, fractals, self-similarity.

Cluster: Fractal Automata

Top

(Use this page for "Sierpinski Bricks.")

Brackets

If you see three yellow blocks together, or the pattern yellow-red-red, color the block above the middle block red.

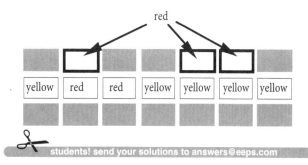

Brackets

If you see three red blocks together, or the pattern yellow-yellow-red, color the block above the middle block yellow.

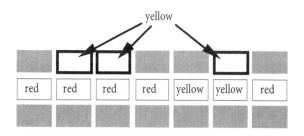

Brackets

If you see the pattern yellow-red-yellow, or the pattern red-yellow-red, color the block above the middle block red.

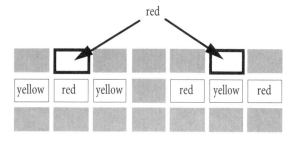

Brackets

If you see the pattern red-yellow-yellow, color the block above the middle block yellow. If you see the pattern red-red-yellow, color the block above the middle block red.

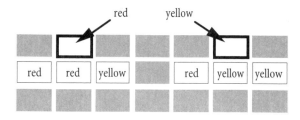

Brackets

Everybody should read this before you each read your own clues.

In this activity, you're going to color in a brick wall according to certain rules. You will color a brick *red* or *yellow* depending on the colors of the bricks below it. Your group can substitute any two colors as long as you agree. You'll need five crayons or marking pens—two yellows, and three reds.

At the beginning, color the far-left and far-right colums red, as indicated on the mat. (This instruction takes care of the "edge rule" in the problem *Sierpinski Bricks*.)

Color the bottom row all yellow, or, if you're adventurous, color a few of them red.

from *United We Solve*　　　　　　　　　　copyright © 1996 by eeps media

Discrete math, fractals.　　　　　　　　**Cluster: Fractal Automata**

Top

color this column red

color this column red

45

(Use this page for "Brackets.")

Nim Games

Materials: scratch paper, pencils, manipulatives

Math: discrete math, optimization, strategy, generalizing from patterns

In a typical Nim game, two players take turns taking things away until no one can move. Ordinarily, the last person to move wins; the person who cannot move loses. Usually this is because there are no more things to take. The other case—where the last person to move *loses*, is often called *poison* or *misère* Nim.

In a typical lesson, the students are challenged to decide whether they want to go first or second, and to come up with a winning strategy.

The purpose of these "problems" is to give students a way to learn the rules of a game without the teacher telling them. You, as the teacher, may have any number of goals:

* You want students to play the game and analyze it to determine whether they want to go first or second;

* you want students to invent their own Nim games, and need a model or two to suggest what you have in mind;

* you want to give students the experience of learning a game from something written rather than by example.

You may want to play a traditional Nim game (for example, *Balloon Ride* from FAMILY MATH) before doing these problems. Many of these games are adapted from *Winning Ways*. (E. R. Berlekamp, J. H. Conway, and R. K. Guy, 1982. London: Academic Press. Two fabulous, formidable volumes.)

Sometimes, groups get hung up trying to figure out how to play a game with four people. Really, these are two-player games. If they don't figure that out, have them play two against two, discussing their moves, or in two one-against-one pairs, discussing the game afterwards or switching opponents.

The "Best Move" Confusion

Sometimes, students get confused about probability and strategy. Suppose they play a game ten times, and eight times the person who went first wins. Often, they'll claim that the person who goes first has "an 80% chance of winning." Or you ask, "Suppose you start with five blocks. Does the first person win or lose?" and they respond, "It depends on what the other person does."

In these games (except *Two Dice 21*) it *doesn't* depend. A winning position means that if you always make your best move, you'll win every time—no matter how well the other person plays. There's no probability about it: it's destiny. You can blow it, of course, and make a poor move. But a complete strategy for one of these games is one that prescribes a "best" move in every possible situation. In a way, these games are not competitive at all. You and your partner work together to make the game as well-played as possible.

Some students need a little time to let this sink in. Let them work it out, asking leading questions:

* In this simple situation, would you rather go first or second?

* Is it still *possible* to lose from this position? (Yes.) If you played it, would you lose? (No. I wouldn't blow it.)

* What's a strategy?

Other General Questions

- Did you find any situations where you knew you had lost?
- Could you play this game with more than two players?

Nim Two Three

The traditional, simplest Nim game (e.g., the one called *Balloon Ride* in FAMILY MATH) lets you take one or two from the pile. But what if you're not allowed to take one? How does that change the strategy?

Tuppins

A variant on traditional Nim. The special rule is that if you take two blocks, they have to be adjacent. And this is an example of *misère* Nim: you lose if you take the last block. Interestingly, there is a symmetry strategy for the "straight" version of this game that lets the first person win easily (Hint: on your first move, take the middle two blocks).

Grundy's Game

This is an amazingly subtle game, but there are only a couple of places where people get confused about the rules. First, you may not split a pile into two equal piles. If there's a pile of six, you can't split it 3-3. Second, when it's your turn, you may split *any one* of the piles on the table (though not into equal piles), no matter how it was created.

Example: Suppose we start with ten. I split it 6-4. You may split the six or the four. Suppose you split the six 4-2. Now we see 4-4-2. I can't split the two (the only way will make two equal piles) but I may split either of the fours. Okay?

The clues ask students to develop a winning strategy that "should include a way to decide the best move in any situation." You may decide how elaborate or comprehensive this should be; it will depend on the age and organizational skills of the students.

After students really know the game, and have solved the game with seven beans, challenge them to move to higher numbers of beans. Persistent students will discover that the obvious pattern does *not* hold.

- How can you tell when the game is over? (There are only ones and twos.)
- How did your group describe the game situations? (Many use numbers in piles, e.g., '2-2-5'.)

Two Dice 21

This is an unusual Nim game because it incorporates randomness. Students steeped in other Nim games can feel frustrated because no one strategy guarantees a win. You might discuss this in debriefing. You might also discuss what a strategy might mean in this game. One way to describe a strategy is to specify, for any number of blocks, how many you would like to take if you get the rolls you want. A more complete strategy would have alternatives if the dice don't behave for you.

NetNim

Each group needs two copies of the NetNim board (page 52) and two markers in order to play this game.

Players take turns moving a marker from the "Start" circle towards a "You win!" circle. Whoever gets there wins.

A hint on clue △ suggests that students figure out which are "good" and "bad" spaces. It should be up to the students to decide what this means. Some groups decide that a "good" space is one that's good to move to. Others decide that a good space is one that's good to be on at the beginning of the move. Still other groups don't realize that some people are saying the opposite of others. This is a good lesson in defining your terms and understanding that mathematicians invent terms to accomplish a purpose. (In *Winning Ways*, the authors label the spaces P- or N-positions depending on whether the advantage goes to the Previous or Next player.)

This game is *isomorphic* to *Nim Two Three*. That is, the strategies are identical; the arrows on the board correspond exactly to subtracting two or three. We have labeled the circles with numbers in order to facilitate students' drawing this conclusion. If students understand this, they can use the network representation of a game to analyze other Nim games such as *Tuppins*. The trick is that a circle represents a *position* in the game, not [necessarily] a number of blocks. So part of a *Tuppins* network might look like this:

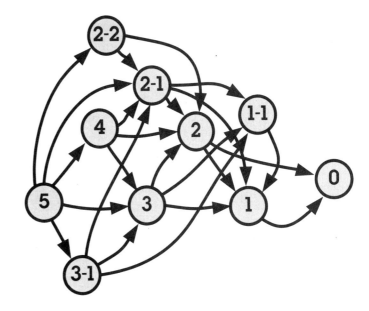

⌃ Nim Two Three

When it is your turn, you may take two blocks, but never just one.

This is a two-player game. Do you want to move first or second?

✂

◂ Nim Two Three

When the game begins, there are ten blocks on the table.

Your job, as a group, is to learn to play the game. Then decide whether you would rather move first or second.

○ Nim Two Three

The game is over if there is only one block left. If it's your turn, you can't move—so you lose.

Do you want to move first or second?

from *United We Solve*

Discrete math, strategies. Starter.

⌄ Nim Two Three

When it is your turn, you may take three blocks, but never four or more.

This is a two-player game. Do you want to move first or second?

▸ Nim Two Three

If you cannot move, you lose the game.

Your job, as a group, is to decide whether you would rather move first or second.

△ Nim Two Three

If it is your turn and there are three blocks left, you can win by taking them all.

You should always assume that the other person will make the best possible move.

Cluster: Nim Games

Tuppins

Tuppins is a two-player game. On your move, you must take at least one block.

Your job, as a group, is to learn the game and figure out whether you would rather go first or second in this game—and why.

Tuppins

On your move, you may take two blocks as long as they are right next to each other.

Your job, as a group, is to learn the game and figure out whether you would rather go first or second in this game—and why.

49

Tuppins

This game begins with eight blocks in a row, right next to each other.

Your job, as a group, is to learn the game and figure out whether you would rather go first or second in this game—and why.

Tuppins

Tuppins is a two-player game. You may not take more than two blocks in your turn.

If you take the last block, you lose.

Your job, as a group, is to learn the game and figure out whether you would rather go first or second in this game—and why.

Tuppins

If it is your turn, and you are faced with four blocks in a row, you're doomed.

On the other hand, if it is your turn, and you are faced with *five* blocks in a row, you can win by taking the middle one.

Tuppins

Extension: What if more than two people played this game? How would that affect your strategy?

Another extension: What if you *won* when you took the last block? How would that change your strategy?

from *United We Solve*

Discrete math, strategies.

Cluster: Nim Games

▲ Grundy's Game

The game begins with a pile of seven beans.

Your group's first job is to use these rules to learn how to play the game.

Your second job is to figure out the best strategy to use.

▼ Grundy's Game

On your move, you must split one pile of beans into two piles.

Your group's first job is to use these rules to learn how to play the game.

Figuring out a strategy includes deciding whether you want to go first or second.

◄ Grundy's Game

You may not split a pile of beans into two equal piles.

Your group's first job is to learn how to play this game. Then you'll need to find a winning strategy. It should include a way to decide the best move in any situation.

► Grundy's Game

You may not cut any of the beans!

If you cannot move, you lose.

Your group's first job is to learn how to play this game. Then you need to figure out a good strategy.

○ Grundy's Game

If there is a pile of four beans, the only move you can make with it is to split it into piles of one and three.

When you figure out your strategy for seven beans, be sure you can explain it.

Extension: What about eight beans? Nine?

△ Grundy's Game

If it's your turn and all the piles of beans have either one bean or two, you have lost the game.

Extension: It's impossible for a game to end with piles of one bean each. There must be at least one "two." Why is that?

from United We Solve

copyright © 1996 by eeps media

Discrete math, strategies.

Cluster: Nim Games

50

Two Dice 21

When it is your turn, you must roll two dice.

If you take all of the blocks that are left, you win. What's a good strategy for playing this game?

Two Dice 21

When it is your turn, you must take as many blocks as there are on one of the dice.

But you may take more blocks, up to the sum of both dice.

51

Two Dice 21

When the game begins, there are 21 blocks on the table.

What's a good strategy for playing this game? Does it matter whether you go first or second?

Two Dice 21

If there are not enough blocks for you to take what you have to, you lose the game.

Your job, as a group, is to come up with a good strategy for playing this game.

Two Dice 21

The game isn't over until a player can't move—either because all of the blocks are gone or the player rolled numbers that are too big to let him or her move.

What's a good strategy?

Two Dice 21

If you roll a four and a two, for example, you can take two, three, four, five, or six blocks.

Hint: Because dice are random, no strategy will make you win every time.

from *United We Solve*

Discrete math, probability, strategies.

Cluster: Nim Games

NetNim

At the beginning of the game, place a marker on the circle marked "Start."

There's only one marker in this game; you don't get your own piece.

NetNim

You may move the marker only when it is your turn. You move it along *one* arrow to another circle.

Your job, as a group, is to learn how to play the game. Then decide whether you would like to go first or second.

NetNim

Extension: The board looks like spilled spaghetti. Can your group come up with a better arrangement for the circles and arrows that looks neater?

NetNim

If you move the marker to a circle marked "You win!", then you win.

You may not move backwards.

Your group's task is to learn the game and to decide whether you want to move first or second.

NetNim

On your turn, you must move the marker.

When you're moving the marker, you must stay on the same arrow (no hopping off!).

As a group, figure out how to play NetNim and devise a good strategy for winning the game.

NetNim

Hint: You may discover that certain circles are "good" and "bad" to move to. That might help you figure out whether it's best to go first.

from *United We Solve*

Discrete math, strategies, networks. Starter.

Cluster: Nim Games

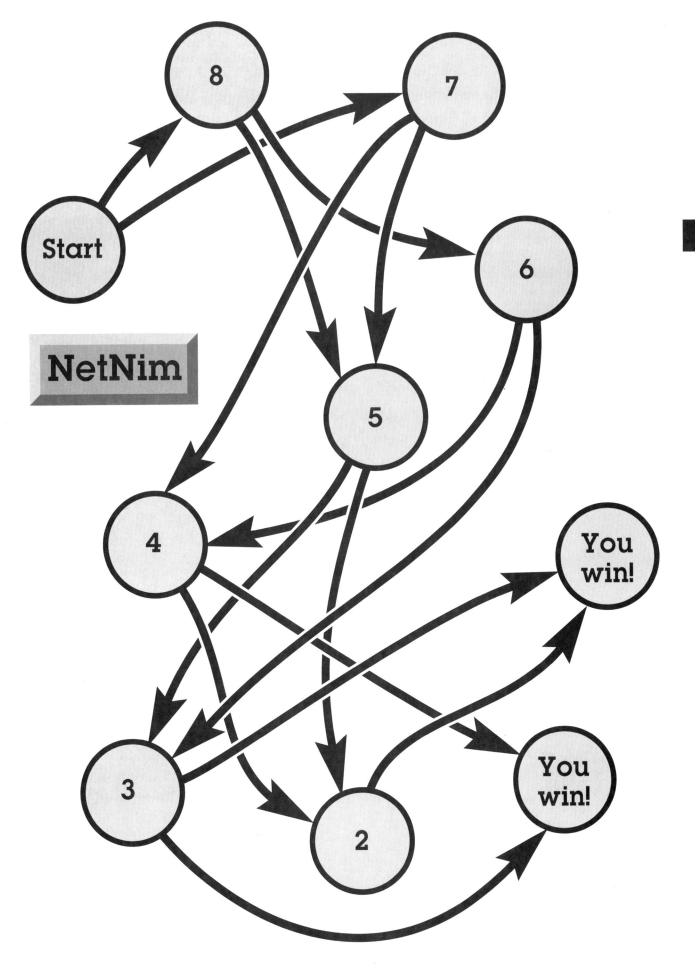

Can You Relate?

Materials: graph paper (master, page 183), pencils, and calculators. *A & P Graph* also requires one sheet of paper for each student and scissors for the group. Groups could use large, 2-cm graph paper to make displays the whole class can see.

Math: scatterplots, statistics, interpolation and extrapolation, reasonableness

These problems are all amenable to solution-by-scatterplot. This does not mean that scatterplots are the only way to solve them; you can make a table and interpolate to do pretty well with *Irena's Gold*, for example. If you do want students to use the plots, though, be sure to provide graph paper!

These problems could be an introduction to scatter plots as well as practice, motivating students to use the tool—especially to help estimate visually the range of possible answers. Ideally, groups will make scatter plots and give as their group response as a range rather than as a single number.

General Questions

- How did your group decide…
- What evidence do you have in order to say…
- Can you get a precise answer?
- How could you simplify these numbers?

Irena's Gold

Lots of names, lots of times, but when the group sorts through the data, they should have a simple table and possibly a graph. You can have them look up the answer in an almanac.

Some groups get hung up with the long names. You might ask in debriefing, "What information is important to solving this problem? What information is extraneous?" Of course, the names are important to history and to the Olympic spirit, but you don't need them to get at the numbers.

The extension in clue △ is a good question to answer as a POW or a short writing assignment.

Golden Arches

The question is whether the number of McDonald's restaurants outside the US will ever exceed those inside, and if so, when. The data come from McDonald's itself.

Students can solve this with a graph or a table. If they are studying linear and exponential growth, they might want to heed clue △ and look at both differences and ratios. Another way to get at this is to use both linear and semi-log graph paper, if they're ready for it.

The extension in clue ○ is a good POW or writing assignment. Students have to make reasonable assumptions and work with proportions and large numbers. You might have students brainstorm questions they need to answer in debriefing, such as, "How much does a hamburger cost?" "How much of the income of a store is in hamburgers?" "What about different-priced hamburgers?"

The Spanish version of this problem, *Arcos Dorados*, is on page 23.

States & Kids

Unlike other problems, these data do not depend on a sequence. You can still use them to interpolate or extrapolate. Look to see what tools the students use. Do they make scatterplots? Do they compute ratios? Do they give answers that are ranges rather than exact numbers?

Less experienced students get stuck when they face some of the large, un-rounded numbers in this problem. In debriefing, you might discuss how many places you need to remember in order to respond to the question.

Data like these can lead to rich investigations. So we have included page 186 with data on a number of interesting variables for the fifty states and D.C. (We apologize to our Canadian colleagues that we did not have suitable data by press time.) For example, suppose you made a ratio of the number of 10-to-14-year olds divided by the number of 40-to-45-year olds. Would that give you an index of the youthfulness of a state? Why is Montana's so high and D.C.'s so low? Why is Florida's not all that low, when they're supposed to have so many old people? (Answer: if you picked 85+ years, you'd see the effect, but baby boomers aren't that old yet!)

The extension in card △ is another chance for a POW or a writing assignment.

NY & LA

This is another extrapolation problem, like *Golden Arches*. It's easier in that it's clearer that LA will catch up, but groups have to deal with larger numbers and use an uneven time scale (the data are not equally spaced).

The clues ask the groups to create a "convincing display that will support" their answer. How elaborate that must be is up to you. It could be a poster, a presentation with an overhead, or just a sheet of paper.

An interesting extension is to ask students to look up these numbers themselves. They will find that different sources give vastly different populations for each metropolitan area. Ask them why they suppose they are different. Even with different numbers, are their conclusions about New York and Los Angeles the same?

A & P Graph

In this problem, each student cuts a piece of (letter-sized) paper into three rectangles, measures the area and perimeter, and plots these two measurements on a group graph. The clues divide the work of making the graph and tell the students the range of each axis.

In that way, this is a more prescribed problem than the others, where the clues give no help with axis-making. On the other hand, the "whole-group" instructions—the large clue at the bottom of the page—give students some discussion topics. Your debriefing would probably be an extension of the questions on that card.

Irena's Gold

In the 1948 Olympics, a woman from the Netherlands won the first women's 200-meter run with a time of 24.40 seconds.

Runners from the USA won the gold in 1960 (24.0 seconds) and 1964 (23.0 seconds).

56

Irena's Gold

Australians have won the women's 200-meter run twice: in the 1952 Olympics, in 23.7 seconds, and in 1956, in 23.4 seconds.

In 1968, Irena Kirszenstein Szewinska, from Poland, won the gold medal in the 200-meter run. Based on your clues, what do you think her time might have been?

Irena's Gold

In 1976 and 1980 Olympics, an East German woman won the gold in the women's 200 m run twice: in 22.37 and 22.03 seconds.

Another East German won in 1972 with a time of 22.4 seconds.

The person who comes in first in an Olympic race wins a gold medal.

Irena's Gold

Runners from the United States won the race in 1984, 1988, and 1992.

Their times were 21.81 seconds, 21.34 seconds, and 21.81 seconds, respectively.

In 1968, Irena Kirszenstein Szewinska, from Poland, won the gold. Work with your group to figure out what her time probably was.

Irena's Gold

When you're all done, you can check your work in an almanac. We used *The Universal Almanac*, published by Andrews and McMeel, the 1993 edition.

Extension: In what year do you think the women will break 20 seconds for this race?

Irena's Gold

Hint: A scatter plot might be a good tool for figuring out Irena's time.

Of course, you won't be able to figure it out exactly, but you might come up with a range that you think is reasonable.

You can add more data from a current almanac.

from *United We Solve*

Interpolation, functions, graphing, Range of answers.

Cluster: Can You Relate?

▲ Golden Arches®

Based on your group's data, do you think there will ever be as many McDonald's in foreign countries as there are in the US? If so, in what year?

McDonald's Restaurants in the US:

year	#
1985	6972
1986	7272
1987	7567
1988	7907
1989	8270

▼ Golden Arches®

Will there ever be as many outside the US as inside?

You and your group should agree on an answer and prepare a graph or chart that supports your convincing argument.

McDonald's Restaurants outside the US:

year	#
1985	1929
1986	2138
1987	2344
1988	2606
1989	2892

◄ Golden Arches®

Will there ever be as many outside the US as inside? When, if ever?

Help your group make a convincing display that will support your answer. A table, chart, or graph might help.

McDonald's Restaurants in the US:

year	#
1990	8576
1991	8764
1992	8959
1993	9283
1994	9744

► Golden Arches®

When (if ever) do you think the number of McDonald's outside the US will catch up with the number inside? Help your group decide. Then make a display that supports your argument.

McDonald's Restaurants outside the US:

year	#
1990	3227
1991	3654
1992	4134
1993	4710
1994	5461

○ Golden Arches®

Extension: in 1994, the average McDonald's that had been open at least one year had $1,800,000 in sales. Wow.

Work with your group and use that figure to estimate the number of hamburgers sold under the golden arches worldwide in 1994. You'll have to make some assumptions.

△ Golden Arches®

Hint: You might approach this problem by looking at the *difference* between the numbers of restaurants inside and outside the US; you might also look at the *ratio* of the numbers. Which makes more sense?

Source: *McDonald's Corporation 1994 Annual Report*. Used with permission.

from *United We Solve*

copyright © 1996 by eeps media

(Spanish version on page 23)
Extrapolation, functions, graphing, range of answers. Group display.   **Cluster: Can You Relate?**

▲ States and Kids

In 1990, Alabama had 4 million people, Montana had 800,000, Massachusetts had 6 million, Wisconsin had 4.9 million, and California had 29.8 million.

How many kids ages 10–14 are there in Illinois? (Don't look it up! Use your group's clues to make an educated guess.)

▼ States and Kids

In 1990, the District of Columbia (D.C.) had 607,000 people, Florida had 12.9 million, Oklahoma had 3.1 million, and Illinois had 11.4 million.

How many kids ages 10–14 are there in Illinois? (Don't look it up! Use your group's clues to make an educated guess.)

◄ States and Kids

In 1990, Alabama had 299,359 kids aged 10–14. D.C. had 29,791, Montana had 63,925, and Florida had 750,410.

How many kids ages 10–14 are there in Illinois? (Don't look it up! Use your group's clues to make an educated guess.)

► States and Kids

In 1990, Massachusetts had 348,379 kids aged 10–14. Oklahoma had 233,167, California had 1,987,011, and Wisconsin had 353,257.

How many kids ages 10–14 are there in Illinois? (Don't look it up! Use your group's clues to make an educated guess.)

○ States and Kids

Hint: There are different ways to go about finding the number of 10–14-year-olds in Illinois. One way is to look at ratios. Another way is to make a scatterplot.

Extension: How accurate do you think your answer is? What is the range of reasonable answers?

△ States and Kids

Extension: How many kids are there in your middle school? Work with your group and use that information to decide how many middle schools you think there are in Illinois or in your state.

Note: the total number of middle schoolers will probably be less than the number of kids aged 10–14.

from *United We Solve*

Interpolation, proportion, graphing, range of answers.

Cluster: Can You Relate?

NY & LA

In 1950, 12.3 million people lived in the New York Metro Area and only 4 million lived in the Los Angeles area. Do you think LA will catch up? If so, when?

A scatter plot may help you and your group make a convincing argument, whatever you decide.

NY & LA

In 1970, 16.2 million people lived in the New York Metro Area and only 8.4 million lived in the Los Angeles area. Based on the information in these clues, do you think LA will catch up? If so, when?

You and your group should agree on an answer and prepare a graph or chart that supports your convincing argument.

NY & LA

In 1990, 16.2 million people lived in the New York Metro Area and only 11.9 million lived in the Los Angeles area. Based on the information in these clues, do you think LA will catch up? If so, when?

Help your group make a convincing display that will support your answer. A table, chart, or graph might help.

NY & LA

In 2000, 16.8 million people will live in the New York Metro Area, while 13.9 million will live in the Los Angeles area.

When (if ever) do you think the population of the Los Angeles area will catch up with New York? Use your clue to help your group decide. Then make a display that supports your argument.

NY & LA

Los Angeles and New York are the two largest metropolitan areas in the U.S. and Canada. (Mexico City is the world's largest.) Do you think the Los Angeles Metropolitan Area will ever have as many people as the New York Metropolitan Area?

NY & LA

A city's "metropolitan area" includes the city itself plus surrounding communities. Los Angeles includes most of the LA Basin, including Orange County. New York's area even includes parts of New Jersey and Connecticut.

from *United We Solve*

Extrapolation, functions, graphing, range of answers. Group display. **Cluster: Can You Relate?**

A & P Graph

You are the **axis-maker**.

Take a sheet of graph paper and make two axes. Label the horizontal axis "perimeter (cm)" and the vertical axis "area (square cm)."

Give the graph to the horizontal-axis scaler.

A & P Graph

You are the **horizontal-axis scaler**.

When you get the graph, put a scale on the horizontal (Perimeter) axis running from 0 cm to 100 cm. Make sure the marks are evenly spaced.

Give the graph to the vertical-axis scaler.

A & P Graph

You are the **vertical-axis scaler**.

When you get the graph, put a scale on the vertical (Area) axis running from 0 cm^2 to 600 cm^2. Make sure the marks are evenly spaced.

Give the graph to the dot supervisor.

A & P Graph

You are the **dot supervisor**.

Ask each person to plot his or her three rectangles in the right places according to their perimeters and areas.

Get your group to work together to be sure it's done right.

A & P Graph

You will need rulers and calculators.

Each of you should do this:
Take a sheet of paper and cut it into three rectangles. Make sure your rectangles are different sizes and shapes. Write the perimeter and area on each one.

Then the **axis-maker** begins.

When the graph is done, discuss:

- What is a rectangle like that belongs in the lower-right corner of the graph?

- Where are the rectangles that are square or nearly square?

- There should be a region where *no* rectangles appear. Why?

from *United We Solve*

Graphing, measurement, area & perimeter, geometry. Group display.   Cluster: Can You Relate?

Growth

Materials: scratch paper, pencils, manipulatives, calculators, graph paper

Math: percentages, compounding, different growth functions, proportion, organizing information

Problems in this cluster are about growth according to several different patterns: linear, quadratic, and especially exponential growth. The latter has to do with proportion and the repeated multiplication of a growth factor. This is also true of shrinking—negative growth—where the factor is often a percentage.

Several problems in the *Can You Relate?* cluster—*Irena's Gold*, *Golden Arches*, and *NY & LA*—are really growth questions as well.

Broken Copier

This problem is OK in sixth grade or late in fifth grade with the two optional clues available up front. Later, most students should be able to get it without the optional clues.

Blue Balls Bounce

There are two kinds of balls, Linyaballs and Proportiaballs. One decays linearly, the other exponentially. The questions ask the group to figure out as much as they can about the patterns of bouncing, comparing the two balls. In particular, which ball bounces higher for which bounces? You should know that the heights cross *twice*: The exponential ball starts and finishes higher than the linear. It may be enough for many students to find the first crossing and see that the exponential decay overtakes the linear decay. You may want to prompt more experienced students to explore further and see where the curves cross again.

- Can you describe exactly what you picture the ball doing each bounce?

Red Balls Bounce

Like Blue Balls Bounce, except backwards. We're told when the two balls bounce the same height and we need to derive the growth (decay) factor for the proportional ball and the increment for the linear ball.

This latter is easier for most students (they divide the 30 cm difference by the 4 bounces to get 7.5 cm per bounce), but students can derive the decay factor by trial and error using the repeat-function feature on most calculators. To test whether 90% is right, for example, press $.9 \times 150 = = = =$, and so forth. Some calculators may ask that you put the repeated factor in last; in that case, reverse the factors.

Found Their Marbles

A variation on the grains-on-a-chessboard situation. Organizing information is important here!

Some students have trouble finding the question. It's on clue ◄.

Mad Scientist

A fun situation that includes tripling-times as well as doubling-times. Many students will stop when they figure out the answer to the nearest hour. That may be fine. With guess-and-check, however, and some repeated-factor calculator work, you can find the "equal" time to any accuracy you like.

⋀ Broken Copier

How do you make a copy the same size as the original?

The copier cannot copy at 100%, but it can copy at 75%.

Work with your group to find as many ways as possible.

⋁ Broken Copier

How do you make a copy the same size as the original?

The copier cannot copy at 100%, but it can copy at 50%.

Work with your group to find as many ways as possible.

◄ Broken Copier

How do you make a copy the same size as the original?

The copier cannot copy at 100%, but it can copy at 400%.

Work with your group to find as many ways as possible.

► Broken Copier

How do you make a copy the same size as the original?

The copier cannot copy at 100%, but it can copy at 133%.

Work with your group to find as many ways as possible.

○ Broken Copier

Hint: You'll have to think about making copies of copies to solve the problem.

How big is a 120% copy of an 80% copy? You can figure it out by multiplying the percentages: $1.20 \times .80 = 96\%$ of the original.

△ Broken Copier

Extension: if your group finds more than one solution, which one do you think will look better when you get done?

from *United We Solve*

Percentages, compounding. Starter.

Cluster: Growth

Blue Balls Bounce

When you drop a blue Linyaball, it will bounce up to the same height except 5 cm less. If you drop it from a height of less than 5 cm, it just doesn't bounce.

On which bounce—or bounces—do the two balls bounce closest to the same height? Work with your group to figure it out.

Do you think real balls bounce more like Linyaballs or Proportiaballs?

Blue Balls Bounce

When you drop a blue Proportiaball, it will bounce up to the same height, except 10 percent less.

Nathan and Julietta drop the balls at exactly the same time.

On which bounce—or bounces—do the two balls bounce closest to the same height?

Work with your group to make an organized graph, table, or chart that shows how the two balls bounce.

63

Blue Balls Bounce

Nathan drops the Proportiaball from a height of 120 cm.

The kids are doing an experiment. They are recording how high the balls bounce.

On which bounce—or bounces—does the Proportiaball bounce higher than the Linyaball? The first bounce is one of them. Work with your group to find them all.

When you do, make an organized graph, table, or chart that shows how the two balls bounce.

Blue Balls Bounce

Julietta drops the Linyaball from a height of 100 cm.

On which bounce—or bounces—does the Linyaball bounce higher than the Proportiaball? Certainly not the first bounce.

You and your group will need a calculator, paper and pencil, and maybe even some graph paper.

Be sure you've looked for all the possible solutions.

Percent, linear vs. exponential, functions.

Cluster: Growth

▲ Red Balls Bounce

When you drop a red Linyaball, it will bounce up to the same height except for a certain number of centimeters less. If you drop it from a height of less than that, it just doesn't bounce.

What is that "certain number of centimeters" for red Linyaballs? Work with your group to figure it out.

Do you think real balls bounce more like Linyaballs or Proportiaballs?

▼ Red Balls Bounce

When you drop a red Proportiaball, it will bounce up to the same height, except a certain percentage less.

Emma and Zoroaster drop the balls at exactly the same time.

What is the "certain percentage less" that the red Proportiaball bounces on every bounce?

Work with your group to make an organized graph, table, or chart that shows how you figured it out.

◄ Red Balls Bounce

Emma drops the Proportiaball from a height of 150 cm.

The kids are doing an experiment. They are recording how high the balls bounce.

Work with your group to make an organized graph, table, or chart that shows how the two balls bounce.

Extension: can you predict the heights for the eighth bounce? Twelfth? Sixteenth?

► Red Balls Bounce

Zoroaster drops the Linyaball from a height of 100 cm.

On the fourth bounce, the two balls bounce to exactly the same height: 70 cm.

You and your group will need a calculator, paper and pencil, and maybe even some graph paper.

Note: there is more than one question you have to answer.

from *United We Solve*

Percent, linear vs. exponential, functions.

Cluster: Growth

▲Found Their Marbles

Every day in April, Alice found a number of marbles equal to ten times the number of the day.

Calvin found two marbles on April 6 (for a total of four). That day, Alice found 60 marbles.

▼Found Their Marbles

Every day in April, Xavier found 100 marbles.

Calvin found one marble on April 4. On that day, Xavier found a hundred marbles for the fourth time—for a total of 400. On that day, Alice found 40 for a total of only 100.

◄Found Their Marbles

On April 1, Calvin found no marbles at all. In fact, he found no marbles on any odd-numbered day.

Here's your group's problem: On which days did Alice have the most marbles altogether? During the first part of April, Xavier had the most.

►Found Their Marbles

On April 2, Calvin found one marble. After that, he found marbles every other day. Strangely, whenever he found some, he found exactly as many marbles as he already had.

At the end of the month, Calvin had the most marbles of any of the kids.

○Found Their Marbles

There are 30 days in April.

Hint: It might help to make a table as you solve this problem. You might also think about what a graph of it would look like.

△Found Their Marbles

Hint: In this problem, you have to keep track of how many marbles each kid finds on each day.

You also have to keep track of the total number of marbles each kid has found.

from *United We Solve*

copyright © 1996 by eeps media

Linear vs. exponential vs. quadratic, functions. Organizing.

Cluster: Growth

Mad Scientist

Elvira the Mad Scientist put 12 mL of disgusting green slime (DGS) into a 1000 mL flask at 12 noon and let it begin to grow.

Will the DGS overflow the flask before midnight?

You and your group will probably need a calculator in this problem.

Mad Scientist

Elvira the Mad Scientist put 1.33 mL of revolting purple slime (RPS) into a 1000 mL flask at 12 noon and let it begin to grow.

Will the RPS overflow the flask before midnight?

Your group will probably need graph paper in this problem.

Mad Scientist

When Elvira checked her cultures at 4:00 PM, there was 48 ML of DGS and 12 mL of RPS.

Elvira is comparing her two slimes, DGS and RPS. Work with your group to determine how fast they grow. And answer the questions on all the cards.

Mad Scientist

When Elvira checked her cultures at 6:00 PM, there was 96 mL of DGS and 36 mL of RPS.

Elvira thinks the RPS will catch up to the DGS by about midnight. She's right. Work with your group to figure out when the two slimes will have equal volumes.

Mad Scientist

Hint: A table might help with this problem. Help your group organize the information.

Look for patterns in the numbers. You might try to figure out what the volumes were at 2:00 PM to check your ideas.

Mad Scientist

Hint: A graph might help you with this problem, to see how the amounts of slime grow and to predict the time they will be equal.

from *United We Solve*

copyright © 1996 by eeps media

Comparing exponential functions. Organizing information. Challenging.   **Cluster: Growth**

Open

In a traditional math problem, there is one way you're meant to address the problem, and you know when you've reached the end. This is in stark contrast to real life. Real life problems are open-ended.

Open-ended problems expand problem solving rather than closing it down. An open-ended problem may have one or more of the following attributes:

- It may have more than one solution. This may be because there is a range of possible answers or because there really are several distinct possibilities. Or the question may be fuzzy or have to do with personal preferences.

- There may be more than one way to approach the problem. Perhaps there is more than one way to represent the information in a problem, or more than one technique for getting to a solution. Often, different students address a problem with different tools.

- There may be work to do even after the problem is solved, often in the form of an extension; or there may be ways to interpret the problem that make it more realistic or challenging. We might call this "open at the top."

Looking at these three attributes, "open-ended" isn't a very good name. Sometimes these problems are "open-middled" or "open-beginninged." So let's just call them "open."

As teachers helping to facilitate work on these open problems, it's important that we remain as open as the problems themselves. We often insist that students solve problems as we would, because our way is faster or snazzier. But is it a good way for that child? We may think that a side-by-side box plot is the very thing for a set of data, but Anna may come across something else that will communicate *her* ideas just fine.

And encourage students to keep going. Students—especially students from traditional programs—can get impatient with open problems because they can't see where to start or they can't tell when they're done. Ideally, students are done when they have done their best work, however far that has led.

The problems in this broad category vary in openness, and they vary in why they were included here. Many problems from the other categories are open to one degree or another as well.

Calculator Equations

Materials: scratch paper, pencils, one four-function calculator (with square root key) per group

Math: number, basic operations, calculator use

The group has a goal number to produce on the calculator, but each member is allowed (or required) to touch only certain keys a certain number of times. The group has to figure out in what order to press the keys to reach the goal. Each problem has more than one solution.

There are some common misunderstandings of the rules to these problems. You can let them work themselves out; but in case you want to clarify, students *are* expected to pass the calculator around and they are *not* allowed to press any of their keys more than once per solution. So if you have a "2," and you press it, and hand it to Eloise, she may have a "2," in which case she may press it and hand it back to you. Then you may not press your "2" again.

Extension: have groups develop their own questions and challenge other groups to solve them. You may even want to insist that they require a particular key (such as the percent key) in their problem.

This cluster of problems is inspired by the game *Equations* by Layman Allen, published long ago by Wff 'n' Proof.

Get Seventeen

This is the easiest of the set, and has no required keys. One clarification: on clue 1, for example, the student does not have to press *both* "times" and "one." Technically, we should say, "You may press only times *or* one," but that may give the impression that the student cannot press both.

One solution: $4 \times 5 - 2 - 1 =$.

Get Ten

There are several solutions (I'm sure we haven't found them all) but here are two sneaky ones that break set:

$2 \times 2 \times 2 + 2 -$ (not ending with the equals key)

$6 - \times 2 + 2\,2 =$ (using the number "22")

- What did you have the most trouble with as you were solving this problem?

Get Five

Clue 4 requires the square root key. There are at least four different solutions, each using the square root key on a different number. (Whence the oblique hint, "radically different.")

An easy one is $9 \sqrt{\ } + 3 - 1 =$

- How did your group use the square root?

- What strategies did you use for finding solutions?

Get One

There are "cheap" solutions that use the decimal point as a throwaway, such as "$7 + 5 \, . \div 4 - 2 =$." More interesting solutions use the decimal point really as a decimal point. You may require that if you wish ("The key following the decimal point must be a digit."), or simply poll the class for such solutions in debriefing. Then issue a challenge to use the key as a genuine decimal point.

- How did your group use the decimal point?

Get Seventeen

Your group's task is to work together to make seventeen (17) show on your calculator. You have to start with it cleared.

You may press only

 and

and you may press each key only once. You do not have to press them in that order. You do not have to press them both.

Other members of your group are allowed to press different keys. You will have to pass the calculator around.

Get Seventeen

Your group's task is to work together to make seventeen (17) show on your calculator. You have to start with it cleared.

You may press only

 and

and you may press each key only once. You do not have to press them in that order. You do not have to press them both.

Other members of your group are allowed to press different keys. You will have to pass the calculator around.

Get Seventeen

Your group's task is to work together to make seventeen (17) show on your calculator. You have to start with it cleared.

You may press only

 and

and you may press each key only once. You do not have to press them in that order. You do not have to press them both.

Other members of your group are allowed to press different keys. You will have to pass the calculator around.

Get Seventeen

Your group's task is to work together to make seventeen (17) show on your calculator. You have to start with it cleared.

You may press only

 and

and you may press each key only once. You do not have to press them in that order. You do not have to press them both.

Other members of your group are allowed to press different keys. You will have to pass the calculator around.

from *United We Solve*

Number, operations. Multiple solutions. Starter.

Cluster: Calculator Equations

Get Ten

Your group's task is to work together to make ten (10) show on your calculator. You have to start with it cleared.

You *must* press

at some point, and you *may* press

You may press each key only once. Other members of your group are allowed to press different keys. You will have to pass the calculator around.

Get Ten

Your group's task is to work together to make ten (10) show on your calculator. You have to start with it cleared.

You *must* press

at some point, and you *may* press

You may press each key only once. Other members of your group are allowed to press different keys. You will have to pass the calculator around.

Get Ten

Your group's task is to work together to make ten (10) show on your calculator. You have to start with it cleared.

You *must* press

at some point, and you *may* press

You may press each key only once. Other members of your group are allowed to press different keys. You will have to pass the calculator around.

Number, operations. Multiple solutions.

Get Ten

Your group's task is to work together to make ten (10) show on your calculator. You have to start with it cleared.

You *must* press

at some point, and you *may* press

You may press each key only once. Other members of your group are allowed to press different keys. You will have to pass the calculator around.

from *United We Solve*

Cluster: Calculator Equations

Get Five

Your group's task is to work together to make five (5) show on your calculator. You have to start with it cleared.

You *must* press

at some point, and you *may* press

You may press each key only once. Other members of your group are allowed to press different keys. You will have to pass the calculator around.

Get Five

Your group's task is to work together to make five (5) show on your calculator. You have to start with it cleared.

You *must* press

at some point, and you *may* press

You may press each key only once. Other members of your group are allowed to press different keys. You will have to pass the calculator around.

71

Get Five

Your group's task is to work together to make five (5) show on your calculator. You have to start with it cleared.

You *must* press

at some point, and you *may* press

You may press each key only once. Other members of your group are allowed to press different keys. You will have to pass the calculator around.

Get Five

Your group's task is to work together to make five (5) show on your calculator. You have to start with it cleared.

You *must* press

at some point, and you *may* press

You may press each key only once. Other members of your group are allowed to press different keys. You will have to pass the calculator around.

from *United We Solve*

Number, operations, square roots. Multiple solutions.

Cluster: Calculator Equations

Get One

Your group's task is to work together to make one (1) show on your calculator. You have to start with it cleared.

You *must* press

at some point, and you *may* press

 and

You may press each key only once. Other members of your group are allowed to press different keys. You will have to pass the calculator around.

Get One

Your group's task is to work together to make one (1) show on your calculator. You have to start with it cleared.

You *must* press

at some point, and you *may* press

You may press each key only once. Other members of your group are allowed to press different keys. You will have to pass the calculator around.

Get One

Your group's task is to work together to make one (1) show on your calculator. You have to start with it cleared.

You *must* press

at some point, and you *may* press

You may press each key only once. Other members of your group are allowed to press different keys. You will have to pass the calculator around.

Get One

Your group's task is to work together to make one (1) show on your calculator. You have to start with it cleared.

You *must* press

at some point, and you *may* press

You may press each key only once. Other members of your group are allowed to press different keys. You will have to pass the calculator around.

from *United We Solve*

Number, operations, decimals. Multiple solutions.   **Cluster: Calculator Equations**

Take It Apart

Materials: scratch paper, pencils, manipulatives

Math: algebra, simultaneous equations

These problems can be solved symbolically, but it's usually easier to solve them with manipulatives, diagrams, or with guess and check. That's just as well; too often students blindly open their algebraic toolbox—and try to fix the watch with a hammer. Then students who don't yet understand symbol manipulation feel stupid when the Brainiac can't solve it, when all they need is a few blocks and common sense.

Some of these problems use larger numbers. If your students use base-ten materials (for example) or use two kinds of manipulatives—beans for ones, blocks for tens, say—they can solve these problems quickly and easily.

Aslan's Fleas

This is a straightforward, single-answer problem accessible to fifth graders. You can use it as a warm-up for older children.

- How did your group represent the fleas?

Chelsea and Aslan

Here we have larger numbers and multiple solutions. In debriefing, ask several groups (that have found only one) for their answers so that students can see there is more than one solution. Then ask for the range of solutions.

- (During) What is the *most* that Bengt can weigh? What if he weighed 200 pounds? Is that possible?

- Does this sound like a good way to weigh pets?

- Suppose you knew that Bengt and Minh together weighed 232 pounds. *Then* could you tell all the weights?

Purple Milk

This problem uses even larger numbers, but you can still use manipulatives (say, a bean for every 25 mL of milk) to solve the problem. But there are multiple solutions—an infinity of them. Oddly, while *Chelsea and Aslan* seems naturally to require only integer solutions, groups solving this problem are more likely to realize that you can have 402.7 mL (and so forth) in one beaker.

The clues ask the groups to "find a way to show all of the solutions to this problem." Students who know about graphs can use them as a tool ("How do the amounts of all the other colors depend on the amount of purple milk?"). But graphs are not necessary.

This problem is related to the *Mixtures* cluster (pages 163–167).

- How is this problem like *Chelsea and Aslan*?

- What are some different ways to show all of the solutions? Is any way better than another?

Balloons (and *Globos*, the Spanish version)

Multiple solutions again, with simple clues. The extra clues let students know there is more than one answer and imply they should find all possibilities.

- What's the smallest number of balloons Hortensia can have?

- How do you know those are all the possibilities?

Aslan's Fleas

Rover has two-thirds as many fleas as Aslan.

Aslan is the only cat in this problem, and he's miserable.

How many fleas does Aslan have?

Aslan's Fleas

If all of Prince's fleas hopped onto Rover, Rover would have 39 fleas.

How many fleas does Aslan have?

Aslan's Fleas

Rover and Spot have 35 fleas between them.

How many fleas does Aslan have?

While Aslan is the True King of Narnia in some books, here, he's an orange-and-white cat.

Aslan's Fleas

If you managed to comb out all of Prince's fleas and all of Spot's fleas, you would have 38 fleas altogether.

How many fleas does Aslan have?

Aslan's Fleas

Spot has the fewest fleas of all the animals.

How many fleas does Aslan have?

Aslan's Fleas

The three dogs together have more than twice as many fleas as Aslan.

How many fleas does Aslan have?

74

from *United We Solve*

Number, algebra, fractions. Starter.

Cluster: Take It Apart

▲ Chelsea & Aslan

Minh held Chelsea on the scale. Together they weighted 146 pounds.

How much do Minh, Chelsea, Aslan, and Bengt weigh individually?

▼ Chelsea & Aslan

When Minh stood on the scale with Aslan, the scale read 121 pounds.

Aslan is a cat.

◄ Chelsea & Aslan

When Bengt held Chelsea on the scale, they weighed 157 pounds.

Chelsea is a dog. She weighs less than four times what Aslan weighs.

► Chelsea & Aslan

When Bengt held Aslan, the scale read 132 pounds.

Bengt weighs more than 120 pounds.

○ Chelsea & Aslan

Bengt and Minh were weighing their pets. They each held each pet while standing on the scale, but they forgot to weigh themselves individually.

Can you figure out how much they weigh?

△ Chelsea & Aslan

All four of them together weigh 278 pounds. But how much do Bengt, Aslan, Chelsea, and Minh weigh individually?

from *United We Solve*

Number, algebra, weight. Multiple solutions.

Cluster: Take It Apart

Purple Milk

If you poured the blue and the red milk together, you would have 800 mL of purple milk.

There are four beakers. Each holds a different color of milk. How much of each color of milk is there?

Purple Milk

If you poured the yellow milk into the white milk, you would have 950 mL of pale yellow milk.

The four beakers each have at least 350 mL of milk to begin with.

Purple Milk

If you poured the red milk and the white milk into the same container, it would have 1000 mL of pink milk. That's one liter.

There is no solution where all four beakers have the same amount.

This problem has many solutions. Work with your group to find a way to show all of the solutions to this problem.

Purple Milk

If you poured the blue milk and the yellow milk together, you'd get green milk—750 mL of it.

How much of each color milk is there?

If you can, show how you know your group found all of the solutions to this problem.

from *United We Solve*

Number, algebra, volume. Multiple solutions.

Cluster: Take It Apart

Balloons

How many balloons does Eric have?

Hortensia has five more than David.

Balloons

How many balloons does Eric have?

David has half as many as Anna.

Balloons

How many balloons does Eric have?

Eric has two fewer than Anna.

Balloons

How many balloons does Eric have?

Hortensia has more than Anna.

Balloons

Hint: You can't determine a single, unique answer for this problem. Your group will have to figure out what you can say *about* the answer.

Balloons

It's impossible for Eric to have 20 balloons.

Hint: It might help to make a table of the possibilities. You could use manipulatives, too.

| Hortensia | Eric | David | Anna |

from *United We Solve*

Number, algebra. Multiple solutions. Organizing. Spanish on page 78.   **Cluster: Take It Apart**

Globos

▲

¿Cuántos globos tiene Eric?

David tiene la mitad de los que tiene Anna.

Globos

▼

¿Cuántos globos tiene Eric?

Hortensia tiene cinco más que David.

Globos

◄

¿Cuántos globos tiene Eric?

Hortensia tiene más que Anna.

Globos

►

¿Cuántos globos tiene Eric?

Eric tiene dos menos que Anna.

Globos

○

Es imposible que Eric tenga 20 globos.

Pista: Les podría ayudar hacer una tabla de las posibilidades. También podrían usar manipulativos.

Globos

△

Pista: Este problema no tiene una respuesta única. Su grupo debe decidir lo que Uds. pueden decir acerca de la respuesta que encontraron.

| Anna | David | Eric | Hortensia |

from *United We Solve*

Number, algebra. Multiple solutions. Organizing. English on page 77.   **Cluster: Take It Apart**

Allocating Scarce Resources

Materials: *lots* of scratch paper, pencils, manipulatives

Math: optimization; discrete mathematics; logic; sequencing; organizing information

These are planning problems. The group has to figure out how to accomplish a task: to schedule or distribute resources to meet some needs. There is no one right way to do these, and no right answer.

There are *better* answers, however: responses that meet more needs, or use elegant, inventive techniques, or communicate the plan more effectively. As such, these problems are perfect for letting groups display their results for others to see and learn from. Have students say what they especially liked about the different displays. The displays are also ideal subjects for student-constructed rubrics.

Testers thought these were some of the most realistic, real-life problems in the book. It's odd that we don't often think of these as "real" math, but planning is squarely in discrete mathematics, an important, up-and-coming subdiscipline. Experience with discrete math in the middle grades—even making sure students realize that these problems *are* mathematics—will be increasingly important in the years to come. The *Networks* cluster (pages 94–99) uses some of the same type of thinking in different contexts.

It's also interesting, watching groups tackle these problems, how much of the work is in organizing the information well. We and our students need plenty of practice.

General Questions

- What would you do differently?
- What makes a plan a good plan?

79

Planning a Play

This problem is mostly about organizing your information. Students can use this year's calendar, or any year's calendar, to develop their timeline. Where there are choices, they will have to decide together on the order of things.

You may want to ask them to prepare a display of their schedule. Since schedules are so important in life and their representations vary so much—from narratives to tables to elaborate graphics—you might have the students look at one another's schedules and say what they especially liked about the different ways of showing what should happen when.

- Do you think these are realistic times for planning a play? (It will depend on the play.)

- Are there other things that should go into the schedule?

- Let's think about a different kind of plan. (Brainstorm events and tasks that need planning, such as Thanksgiving dinner, a party, building a house.) What are the parts of it? Which parts require other parts to be done first?

Carpool

Older students found this pretty easy, but it's still a good task for organizing information. You may want to insist that students come up with a way to display their schedule so all the parents in the problem can understand it.

- How did your group decide what was fair? What did you mean by fair?

Career Day

Once again, this is about organizing information. The task itself is not tricky (students may want to develop a harder version where people's needs are harder to meet), but it takes awhile for the group to agree on a way to process all the information they have. There are no extra clues.

- Did everybody get their first choice?

- What did you do about the people who didn't fill in all their choices?

- Have you ever had to do this in real life?

Moon Base

This is a hybrid problem, a network problem about allocating resources. The information problem is not as serious as in *Career Day*, but representing the solution, and especially deciding what to cut out, are more difficult.

It's fun for groups to see one another's solutions and to see how different they are. This is a good one to let kids present on the overhead.

- What compromises did your group make?

- How did you decide what was most important?

Note:
Why This Is Discrete Mathematics

In the 1991 NCTM *Yearbook, Discrete Mathematics Across the Curriculum, K–12*, John Dossey says that discrete mathematics concerns itself with three kinds of questions:

- Existence (Is there a way to…?)

- Counting (How many ways can you…?)

- Optimization (What's the best way to…?)

This cluster falls in the third category. What's the best way to allocate our resources—time, people, rides, and so forth—to accomplish the task?

The problems are also *discrete*—they concern themselves with separate objects or configurations. The classic what-dimensions-of-a-rectangle-will give-you-the-biggest-area-for-a-given-perimeter problem, in contrast, is *continuous*. It is possible to imagine four and a half meters of fence; you can't arrange four and a half rides or connect four and a half rooms together.

Planning a Play

It will take four weeks to build the scenery, and four weeks to sew and fit the costumes.

The script must be finished before scenery can be designed.

The first dress rehearsal must be at least one week before opening night, which is May 10.

Planning a Play

The scenery and costumes have to be finished before the first dress rehearsal.

You're working on the script now. When does the script have to be done?

The scenery and costumes must be designed before you can start to make them.

Planning a Play

It will take two weeks to design the scenery.

It will take you a week from the time you start holding auditions until you decide who will play which part (that's called casting). You can't design costumes until casting is done.

When do you have to finish the script?

Planning a Play

The script has to be done before you hold auditions.

The actors need six weeks—between casting and the first dress rehearsal—to learn their lines and the blocking.

Costume design takes one week.

Opening night is May 10.

Planning a Play

You and your group have to decide when the script has to be done in order to have enough time to get ready for the first performance on May 10.

Hint: You might want to make a list, table, or diagram showing how long different tasks take.

Planning a Play

Hint: You might want to make a diagram showing which tasks have to be completed before other tasks can begin.

You can use a calendar for this year to figure out the dates, if you wish.

from *United We Solve*

Discrete math, optimization, planning. Realistic context, multiple solutions.   **Cluster: Allocating**

Carpool

Blaise, Kyle, Penelope, and Quincy are in a volleyball league at the Community Center. It's too far to walk, so they decided to ask their parents to drive them. Their parents asked them to arrange a carpool.

Your group's job is to plan it.

Who drives when?

Carpool

Kyle and Penelope are twins (though they don't look it). Their Uncle Max can drive, but only to pick up, and only Thursdays, Fridays, and Saturdays. Their mom can take kids (but not pick up) on Mondays and Tuesdays.

Make the carpool arrangements as fair as you can. You decide what that means.

Carpool

Blaise's mom can drive, either direction, on Wednesdays and Thursdays. She can do Fridays if she really has to but you can tell it would be an inconvenience.

The kids can take the bus, but the route is lousy and takes over an hour.

Carpool

The league plays from 4:00 pm to 7:00 pm Tuesday, Wednesday, Thursday, and Friday, for three weeks. Then there's the final tournament on the last Saturday.

Quincy's Dad can take them at 4:00 on Wednesday and Friday, and can drive both directions on Saturday.

Carpool

Your job, with your group, is to come up with a fair plan for the carpool to the volleyball league.

The hard part in this problem is deciding what's fair. For example, since Kyle and Penelope are brother and sister, should their family drive more?

Carpool

Your job, with your group, is to come up with a fair plan for the carpool to the volleyball league.

There are a total of 26 trips to arrange.

Hint: You might consider making a chart to display your schedule.

from *United We Solve*

Discrete math, optimization, planning, fairness. Realistic, multiple solutions.   Cluster: Allocating

Career Day

Time for Career Day! There are four guest speakers: a chef, a video producer, a computer scientist, and a coroner (that's someone who works with corpses found in suspicious circumstances). The twenty-six kids were asked which three they would most like to attend, though they will attend only two. Here are some of the results:

Name	#1	#2	#3
Hazel	Chef	Cor	Vid
Isaac	Vid	Comp	Cor
Julietta	Cor	Vid	Comp
Kyle	Cor	Chef	Vid
Lobelia	Vid	Comp	Cor
Minh	Vid	Cor	Chef

Career Day

You and your group get to schedule Career Day for twenty-six kids. Each student will attend two sessions: one at 9:00 and one at 10:30. Each session will last eighty minutes. There's a ten-minute break between them.

Here are some of their requests. See if you can make a schedule that's fair to everyone:

Name	#1	#2	#3
Nathan	Vid	Cor	
Oscar	Cor	Vid	Chef
Penelope	Comp	Chef	Cor
Quincy	Cor	Vid	Chef
Ravi	Vid	Cor	Comp
Sofia	Vid	Chef	Cor

Career Day

There are two rooms: Room 17 and Room 22. You need to schedule the speakers and the students. First, two of the speakers will speak, then the other two.

Here are some of the students' choices. Give them their highest choices if you can.

Name	#1	#2	#3
Alice	Vid	Cor	Chef
Blaise	Vid	Chef	Comp
Charlotte	Cor	Vid	Comp
Dwayne	Vid	Comp	
Emma	Cor	Vid	Comp
Felicia	Comp	Vid	Cor
Gustavo	Cor	Comp	Vid

Career Day

Each of the sessions at Career Day can hold thirteen students—fourteen if crowded.

Each speaker speaks only once, but you can decide when.

Here are some of the students' choices, though not everyone picked three:

Name	#1	#2	#3
Tonya	Vid	Cor	Chef
Ursula	Vid	Comp	Cor
Victor	Cor	Comp	Vid
Wayne	Chef	Comp	Cor
Xanthia	Chef		
Yvonne	Vid	Cor	Comp
Zoroaster	Cor	Comp	Vid

from *United We Solve*
copyright © 1996 by eeps media

Discrete math, optimization, fairness. Realistic context, multiple solutions.   Cluster: Allocating

Moon Base

Your group will design the moon base. Meet all the specifications and try to meet as many requests as you can. Try to be fair.

The moon base is made up of circular pods connected by tubes. You have only seven pods, though you were supposed to get ten.

The cook wants a Dining Pod connected to the Kitchen, the Commissary, the Bathroom, and the Dorm; and a Kitchen Pod connected to Dining, Commissary, and the Office.

The original plans called for a Shower & Bathroom pod that also contained the water recycling equipment. That pod is essential.

Moon Base

Your group will design the moon base.

Be sure to meet all the specifications. For example, no tubes may cross.

The Rec Director wants a Games Pod connected to the Dorm, the Library, the Dining pod, and the Commissary; and a Sports Pod (low-gravity handball, very fun) connected to the Showers and the Dorm.

The Commissary is the place where supplies such as food and oxygen tanks get stored.

A connector connects a pod to a tube. That's all it can do.

Moon Base

Your group will design the moon base.

You have only 22 tube connectors (you were supposed to get 36). Each tube, of course, needs two connectors: one on each end.

The Science Director wants the Observatory connected to the Dining pod, the Dorm, and the Library; and she wants the Games Pod far away (the lights from the video games interfere with the telescopes).

You will not be able to give everybody what they want.

A Dorm (Dormitory) is a room where people sleep.

Moon Base

Your group will design the moon base.

Be sure to meet all the specifications. For example, each tube must be straight.

The Personnel Director wants the Dorm Pod connected to the Office Pod, the Showers, and the Dining Pod; and the Office Pod connected to the Dorm, the Library, the Observatory, and the Dining Pod.

The Observatory is the whole point of the moon base. You have to give it its own pod. Since there aren't enough pods, other functions may have to be combined.

from *United We Solve*

Discrete Math, networks, optimization, fairness. Multiple solutions. Drawing.   Cluster: Allocating

Many Faces

Materials: scratch paper, pencils

Math: statistics, multiple representations

This cluster explores the different ways students can represent the same data or processes. In addition to these problems, many others in this book benefit from more than one way of looking at things. You can make any problem in the *Can You Relate?* cluster (pages 54–60) into a member of this one by insisting on more than one display in the groups' responses.

Kids' Heights

This is a "teacher's message" problem. Each student has a different representation of the same data, and a question best answered by the display on some other card. If the group follows the rules and doesn't share their cards, they each get to answer someone else's question. And they get to see that different representations are good at communicating different things.

The cards include a stem-and-leaf plot and a box-and-whisker. Avoid this problem unless your students have seen these two types of graph.

- Which of the questions could you answer from the card with the list of kids and heights?

- Are these heights realistic?

Round Robin

This is the classic handshake problem in another incarnation. Here, the students work as a group to solve the problem, then work together to help each individual create a solution that uses a different method. Seeing four different solutions to the same problem is very powerful.

The clues also ask students to "be sure you see how the features of your solution are reflected in the others." It's up to you to decide how far to take this, but it's good practice for students to analyze the solutions and explain why they are the same.

- Have you ever seen a problem like this before?

- How is this network solution with all the lines the same as this table?

If you use portfolios that can accommodate group work, this is a good task to include.

East & West

We have deliberately left vague how the students are supposed to support their arguments. You may want to leave it this open-ended, or you may want to make a specific instruction depending on what you're teaching. You may, for example, insist that they calculate both the mean and the median in order to see how different they are (they are, with these data); or you may insist that they create box plots or a back-to-back stem-and-leaf—both of which are good for these data.

We have also left out a means of identifying states as eastern or western. A US map is included on page 185 if you want to pass it out.

- How did you decide which states were eastern and western?

- How does your display—or graph, or analysis—make a convincing argument that eastern states have more people than western.

- Suppose somebody said that western states had more. What argument do you think he or she would use to support that claim? (e.g., California is biggest by a lot.)

Kids' Heights

This is a boxplot of some height data for some middle-school students. Are there more girls or boys in this sample?

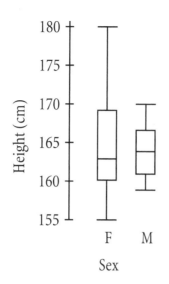

Kids' Heights

Below is a stem-and-leaf plot of some height data for some middle-school students. The heights are in centimeters.

Heights

```
15|5999
16|00111122444566799
17|0015
18|0
```

example: "16|1" means 161 cm

What is the name of the tallest student?

Kids' Heights

Here is some height data for 26 middle-school students:

Name	Height (cm)	Name	Height (cm)
Alice	155	Nathan	159
Blaise	161	Oscar	166
Charlotte	167	Penelope	180
Dwayne	170	Quincy	166
Emma	160	Ravi	161
Felicia	165	Sofia	171
Gustavo	169	Thalia	159
Hazel	162	Ursula	175
Isaac	164	Victor	169
Julietta	164	Wayne	161
Kyle	159	Xanthia	162
Lobelia	160	Yvonne	170
Marianela	161	Zoroaster	164

Which group has the bigger spread in heights—the females or the males?

Kids' Heights

Here is a column chart that shows data about a height study of some middle-school students:

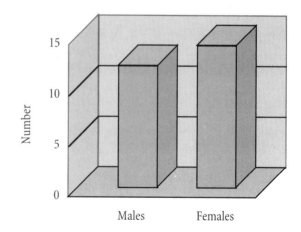

What is the most common height of students in the study?

from *United We Solve*

copyright © 1996 by eeps media

Statistics. Multiple representations. Multiple questions.

Cluster: Many Faces

Round Robin

Get the group to help you make a display that shows how to solve the problem with a *formula* or a *number pattern* that works with different numbers of teams.

You should all get the same answer, of course! When you're done, be sure you see how the parts of your solution appear in the other solutions.

Round Robin

Get the group to help you make a display that shows how to solve the problem with a *diagram* or *network*.

You should all get the same answer, of course! When you're done, be sure you see how the parts of your solution appear in the other solutions.

Round Robin

Get the group to help you make a display that shows how to solve the problem with *manipulatives* or a *systematic list*.

You should all get the same answer, of course! When you're done, be sure you see how the parts of your solution appear in the other solutions.

Round Robin

Get the group to help you make a display that shows how to solve the problem with a *table* or *chart*.

You should all get the same answer, of course! When you're done, be sure you see how the parts of your solution appear in the other solutions.

87

Round Robin

Solve this problem, discuss it with your group, then refer to your individual cards and solve it again. Your job as a group is to make a display that shows four *different* approaches. You work together, of course—but you are in charge of the one referred to on your card.

Six teams play in a round-robin basketball tournament. Each team plays each other team once. How many games are played altogether?

from *United We Solve*

Discrete math. Counting. Multiple representations. Group display.   **Cluster: Many Faces**

East and West

Which tend to have more people: eastern or western states? Work with your group to create at least two ways of supporting your choice mathematically.

```
Alabama ............... 4,040,587
Alaska ................. 550,043
Arizona .............. 3,665,228
Arkansas ............. 2,350,725
California ........... 29,760,021
Colorado ............. 3,294,394
Connecticut .......... 3,287,116
Delaware ............... 666,168
District of Columbia ... 606,900
Florida ............. 12,937,926
Georgia .............. 6,478,216
Hawaii ............... 1,108,229
Idaho ................ 1,006,749
```

Source: *1990 Census STF3 CD-ROM*

East and West

Which states generally have more people: eastern or western? That is, does a typical eastern state have more people than a typical western one?

```
Illinois ............. 11,430,602
Indiana .............. 5,544,159
Iowa ................. 2,776,755
Kansas ............... 2,477,574
Kentucky ............. 3,685,296
Louisiana ............ 4,219,973
Maine ................ 1,227,928
Maryland ............. 4,781,468
Massachusetts ........ 6,016,425
Michigan ............. 9,295,297
Minnesota ............ 4,375,099
Mississippi .......... 2,573,216
Missouri ............. 5,117,073
```

Source: *1990 Census STF3 CD-ROM*

East and West

Which states tend to have more people: eastern or western? Support your choice mathematically at least two ways. One should probably be a graph. You'll also need to decide which states are which.

```
Montana ................. 799,065
Nebraska ............. 1,578,385
Nevada ............... 1,201,833
New Hampshire ........ 1,109,252
New Jersey ........... 7,730,188
New Mexico ........... 1,515,069
New York ............ 17,990,455
North Carolina ....... 6,628,637
North Dakota ........... 638,800
Ohio ................ 10,847,115
Oklahoma ............. 3,145,585
Oregon ............... 2,842,321
Pennsylvania ........ 11,881,643
```

Source: *1990 Census STF3 CD-ROM*

East and West

Which states have more people: eastern or western? You need at least two mathematical supports for your choice. One should be a calculation—comparing means or medians, say. Be able to explain why your calculation is appropriate.

```
Rhode Island .......... 1,003,464
South Carolina ........ 3,486,703
South Dakota ........... 696,004
Tennessee ............. 4,877,185
Texas ............... 16,986,510
Utah ................. 1,722,850
Vermont ................ 562,758
Virginia ............. 6,187,358
Washington ........... 4,866,692
West Virginia ........ 1,793,477
Wisconsin ............ 4,891,769
Wyoming ................ 453,588
```

Source: *1990 Census STF3 CD-ROM*

from *United We Solve*

Statistics. Multiple representations. Group display.

Cluster: Many Faces

Not Enough Info!

Materials: scratch paper, pencils, manipulatives

Math: estimation, proportion, discrete math—it's all over the map!

In these problems, the groups know up front that they do not have enough information to answer the questions. The group has to make some reasonable assumptions. Sometimes, the clues give hints about the kinds of quantities the group might think about.

Other problems in this book have some of the same qualities. *East and West* in the *Many Faces* cluster, for example, requires groups to come to agreement about what is an eastern state and what is western.

Hairy Problem and *CD-ROM* are "back-of-the-envelope" calculations. Both benefit from—but do not require—scientific notation.

Lemonade

This takes a little imagination and calculation, and can result in quite a wide range of answers. The open-endedness can be a challenge for students if they're not used to it. A discussion beforehand about how to make lemonade might orient the students to the process.

Overnight Hike

This is more challenging. Groups have to know a little about rates (e.g., How long does it take to hike three miles at two miles per hour?). They also have to figure out how long it will take to get everybody across Weasel Lake (I can do it in less than an hour and a half.).

- How did your group handle getting across Weasel Lake?

CD-ROM

This is a good "back-of-the-envelope" calculation. It would also work well as a POW, and a written response could be a portfolio piece.

Groups are asked to figure out how many CD-ROMs it would take to store all the text (not the pictures) in their school library. Each clue gives some useful information and poses some questions the group may need to answer in order to come up with a final response. Students solving this problem could use scientific notation, though it isn't necessary.

The underlying proportions involve multiplying the right quantities together; for example, to find the number of words in a book, multiply the number of pages in the book by the number of words on a page.

- How many books do you think are in our library?" (Note: you don't have to know this to answer the question. Some groups just measure shelf length.)
- Why do you suppose we don't have our whole library on CD-ROM(s)?

For many libraries, the answer is "1."

A Hairy Problem

Imagine that you could collect all the hair cut around the country—in barber shops, fancy salons, kitchens, anywhere—for an entire year and splice it end to end. How long would the resulting hair be?

Clues give some useful information and suggest some considerations to the students. Many students get snarled in worrying about fine distinctions. This problem may help get them into the back-of-the-envelope spirit. If you're worried, though, ask (beforehand, or while students are working): "How accurately do you think we need to know the answer?"

This is an even more open-ended problem than *CD-ROM*, and it benefits even more from scientific notation. The numbers get so large that they overflow most calculators; this may be a good lesson. Alternatively, you can alter the clues before you photocopy the problem: add information on the U. S. population, eliminate the suggestion that blondes have more hairs than other people, and so forth. You could make the numbers smaller by restricting the problem to your town instead of using the whole country—though the resulting distances will not be as astronomical.

- How far is that compared to the distance to the moon? How far is it compared to the distance to the Sun?
- If you had a penny for every hair on everyone's head in the United States, how much money would you have? Is that more or less than the national debt? (It's much less.)

Lemonade

Thalia and Sofia decided to open a lemonade stand to make some money.

They borrowed a card table from Thalia's mom and two folding chairs from Sofia's Aunt Mel.

You and your group will need to agree to make some assumptions in order to finish this problem.

Lemonade

Thalia and Sofia needed a sign, some sugar, lemons, pitchers, ice, paper cups, and napkins. And a table and a couple of chairs.

How much money did they make after they had paid for the things they had to buy?

Lemonade

Thalia's next-door neighbor has a lemon tree and lets Thalia pick as many lemons as she wants.

It was a very hot day, and they sold 58 cups of lemonade.

Lemonade

Sofia and Thalia borrowed pitchers from their homes.

Sofia's dad said they could buy paper cups from him for 3¢ each.

How much money did they make?

Lemonade

Here are some things you might want to decide:

What do you think is a reasonable price for a cup of lemonade on a hot day?

Will they have materials for making a sign, or will they have to buy something?

Lemonade

Here are some things you may want to think about:

If they can't get sugar from home, how much do you think it will cost?

Is 3¢ a reasonable price for a paper cup? How much would it cost for them to buy some at the store?

from *United We Solve*

copyright © 1996 by eeps media

Number, money. Multiple solutions, realistic context.

Cluster: Not Enough Info!

Overnight Hike

Lobelia and Ravi are planning an overnight hike for 24 kids from their school.

Tonya told them they shouldn't plan on hiking faster than two miles per hour with such a large group.

An experienced rower can row across Weasel Lake in about 6 minutes.

Overnight Hike

The campsite is three miles from the trailhead (that's where you have to stop driving and start walking). That doesn't count the lake they have to cross.

Lobelia, who rows a lot, says that a typical rowboat will carry three kids and their stuff.

How long will it take to get everybody to the campsite?

Overnight Hike

On the way, they need to cross Weasel Lake (it's long and skinny—too far to go around). Ravi called ahead and learned that there are two rowboats they could use.

How long will it take to get everybody to the campsite? You'll have to make some assumptions; be sure you know what they are!

Overnight Hike

The rule on the rowboats is that you have to leave them so that there is one rowboat on each side of the lake. And that's the way the kids will find them.

You and your group will have to make some assumptions. For example, how many people are good rowers? Will they get tired?

Overnight Hike

Here are some things you might want to decide:

What's a reasonable length of time for an inexperienced rower to cross Weasel Lake? What if two people were rowing? Is it worth using both boats?

Overnight Hike

Here are some things you may want to think about:

How long will it take just to get people organized when it's time to get into the boats? That time isn't included in the rowing time. Or can some people just start rowing while the others get organized?

from *United We Solve*

copyright © 1996 by eeps media

Number, time, speed. Multiple solutions, realistic context.

Cluster: Not Enough Info!

CD-ROM

How many CD-ROMs would it take to store all the words in your school library?

You will have to make some sensible estimates to help your group figure this out. Here is some information that might help:

In 1996, a CD-ROM can hold about 600,000,000 (six hundred million!) characters (or bytes) without compression.

And here is a question you might want to ask yourself along the way:

How would you estimate the number of pages in a typical book?

CD-ROM

How many CD-ROMs would it take to store all the words in your school library?

You will have to make some sensible estimates to help your group figure this out. Here is some information that might help:

To store the text (not the pictures) of a book, each letter and space in the entire book counts as one character.

And here is a question you might want to ask yourself along the way:

How would you estimate the number of words on a typical page?

CD-ROM

How many CD-ROMs would it take to store all the words in your school library?

You will have to make some sensible estimates to help your group figure this out. Here is some information that might help:

If you use compression, you can fit more data onto CD-ROMS. You can typically save 30%—and as much as 80%—of the space the data would have taken.

And here is a question you might want to ask yourself along the way:

How many books are on a typical shelf in your library?

CD-ROM

How many CD-ROMs would it take to store all the words in your school library? For this problem, just think about the words. Pictures take up a lot more space.

You will have to make some sensible estimates to help your group figure this out. Here are some questions you might want to ask yourself along the way:

How would you estimate the number of characters in a typical book?

How would you estimate the number of books in your school library?

---

from *United We Solve*

Large numbers, scientific notation. Multiple solutions, realistic context. Cluster: Not Enough Info!

A Hairy Problem

If you could take a year and splice together all the hair that is cut in this country, how long would the hair be? Work with your group to figure it out.

Your group's response may, in the end, turn out to be a range of answers rather than a single number.

Here is a question you may want to ask along the way: Does it matter if your hair is curly?

You may want to estimate, or do a survey, or look up an answer.

One barber we talked to said that hair grows about 12 mm a month.

A Hairy Problem

If you collected all the hair that is cut in this country for a whole year—in parlors, barber shops, kitchens, everywhere—and spliced it together, how long would the hair be? Work with your group to figure it out.

Here is a question you may want to ask along the way: How many people are there in the country?

You may want to estimate, or do a survey, or look up an answer.

One barber we talked to said that hair grows about 4 mm a week. How fast does *your* hair grow?

A Hairy Problem

If you could splice together all the hair that is cut in this country over an entire year, how long would the hair be? Work with your group to figure it out.

One strategy is for each group member to do this problem separately, then compare your answers.

Here is a question you may want to ask along the way: How many hairs are on a typical head? Do you think you could figure it out?

Extension: the distance from the Earth to the Sun is about 150,000,000 kilometers. How does that compare to the hair?

A Hairy Problem

Imagine collecting all the hair that is cut in this country for an entire year, and then splicing it all together into one long hair. How long would that hair be? Work with your group to figure it out.

Here is a question you may want to ask along the way: How much does hair grow in a year?

You may want to estimate, or do a survey, or look up an answer.

One hair stylist told us that a typical brunette has about 120,000 hairs, but that a blonde has quite a few more. There is a lot of variation, though.

from *United We Solve*

Large numbers, growth, scientific notation. Multiple solutions.   **Cluster: Not Enough Info!**

Networks

Materials: scratch paper, pencils

Math: discrete math, graph theory, multiple
              representations, optimization

In this cluster, groups construct a network (or *graph* in the discrete-math sense) and answer a question based on that network. The clues are about the nodes and connections; the group has to make a representation of the whole network. You can represent a network using dots (or blobs) for the nodes and lines for the connections. There are other ways, too.

Some traditional network questions (e.g., the Königsberg Bridges problem) are *Euler Path* questions (after the famous mathematician)—ones that ask if it's possible to travel every route without backtracking. Other network questions ask for *optimization*—they ask for the fastest or cheapest or shortest route around the network. Problems in this cluster represent both types.

Moon Base (page 84) in the *Allocating Scarce Resources* cluster is also a network problem.

Floating City

Each clue contains connections between different barges that make up the city. Each group makes a map of the network of barges. If groups compare them, they will look different. Nevertheless, the maps will be the same in terms of their connections; they will be *isomorphic*.

Students may want to make labels. Because sticky notes are so good for this problem, we did not make labels for you.

In debriefing, you can include questions about the group's process, their use of manipulatives, and about the extensions on clues 5 and 6.

The Dozen Eggs

There are really two tasks here: to figure out the layout of the Underground Mansion, and then to find a path through the mansion that uses each corridor only once. This is an *Euler path* problem. In this case, it's possible. In Königsberg, it isn't.

- How did you and your group decide how to draw the map?

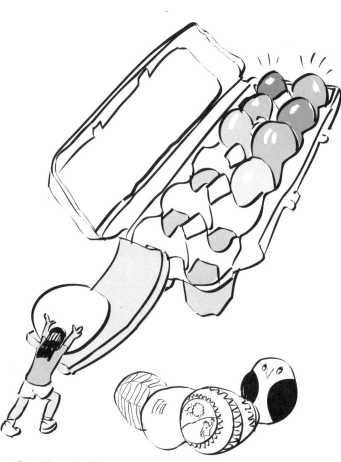

Snake Lake

Clues are road signs showing mileages. The task is twofold again: to make the map, and then use it to find the shortest route from Eastlake Village to Westlake Village. Kids have an easier time with this than adults. Sticky notes are useful for this problem. If you're in Canada, distances are in kilometers.

- How did you decide you had found the shortest route?

- How did you figure out the distance from ... to ...?

Whittle County

This is an elaborate situation for experienced, enthusiastic problem solvers. At first, the information is confusing. Organizing it is hard. But there really are some common-sense strategies you can apply to try to find the quickest route. So far, Julie Bagniefsky holds the record.

▲ Floating City

Work with your group to draw a map of the city.

There are causeways connecting Carp Condos to the Library; Spindrift Villas to the museum; and City Hall to the Market.

▼ Floating City

In your map, all of the causeways must be straight.

City Hall is connected directly to five other barges. Three of them are the Carp Condos, the Fat Albatross, and the Library.

◄ Floating City

The floating city is made up of barges connected by causeways. The causeways may not cross.

Six causeways connect The Portside School to six places: the museum, the Spindrift Villas, the Library, Carp Condos, the Market, and even City Hall.

► Floating City

Each barge has a building or a particular function.

The Can What We Can Fish Company occupies one barge. It's the city's main employer. It's connected to the Spindrift Villa Apartments, the Market, and the Fat Albatross restaurant.

○ Floating City

Hint: If your map doesn't work out, you might try writing the names of the barges on slips of paper.

Extension: Nemo lives in Spindrift Villas and would like to be able to visit every barge without visiting any barge twice. His sister says it's impossible. What do you think?

△ Floating City

Extension: Suppose you were going to add one causeway. Where would you put it to most improve the way the barges are connected?

Suppose you had to remove one? Which one would do the least harm? The most?

from *United We Solve*

copyright © 1996 by eeps media

Discrete math, maps. Multiple solutions.

Cluster: Networks

95

There is one egg in each of the twelve corridors in Baroness Ursula Ulrich's Underground Mansion. Each egg is of a different stone. The complete set would be indescribably valuable.

The garnet egg is in the corridor between the Game Room and the Grand Foyer.

The amethyst egg is in the corridor between the Torture Chamber and the Study.

The diamond egg is in the corridor between the Kitchen and the Pantry.

What route do you want to take through the Mansion?

There is one egg in each of the corridors in Baroness Ursula Ulrich's Underground Mansion. Collect all twelve!

The ruby egg is in the corridor between the Equipment Room and the Grand Foyer.

The crystal egg is in the corridor between the Dining Room and the Study.

The sapphire egg is in the corridor between the Kitchen and the Dining Room.

What route can you take through the mansion so you can get all twelve eggs?

The emerald egg is in the corridor between the Dining Room and the Grand Foyer.

The alabaster egg is in the corridor between the Torture Chamber and the Kitchen.

The opal egg is in the corridor between the Equipment Room and the Study.

Collect all twelve eggs. You need to decide on a route, but you also need to decide what room you want to start in and what room you want to end in (You'll get out through a skylight. But once you leave, you can't go back in).

Baroness Ursula Ulrich's Underground Mansion is in such terrible shape that every time you walk through a corridor and collect an egg, the corridor collapses so you can't ever use it again.

The lapis egg is in the corridor between the Study and the Grand Foyer.

The granite egg is in the corridor between the Game Room and the Dining Room.

The topaz egg is in the corridor between the Dining Room and the Pantry.

There are eight rooms in the mansion, but there are no eggs in the rooms—only in the corridors.

from United We Solve

Discrete math, Euler paths, maps. Multiple solutions.   **Cluster: Networks**

Snake Lake

Here is a sign in Northside (facing south):

⬆ Evans Bridge — Southport **2**
➡ [16] WEST — Oakpointe **3**
⬅ [16] EAST — Abernathy **7**

Snake Lake is long and thin, winding more or less east and west. It has two bridges: the Evans Bridge, and the Snake Lake Causeway.

Snake Lake

Here is a sign in Eastlake Village, showing the distances along two different highways to Westlake Village:

➡ [16] WEST — Westlake Village **21**
⬅ [14] WEST — Westlake Village **23**

Two highways connect Eastlake Village to Westlake Village. Highway 16 winds along the north shore of the lake, while Highway 14 winds along the south shore.

Snake Lake

Here is a sign in Evans Cove (facing north):

⬆ Snake Lake Causeway — Oakpointe **2**
➡ [14] EAST — Southport **9**
⬅ [14] WEST — Westlake Village **5**

It will be useful to make a map or diagram— with distances—to show your route.

Snake Lake

In this problem, you and your group must find the shortest route from Westlake Village to Eastlake Village. Your clues are in the form of road signs, such as this one along Highway 16 in Abernathy.

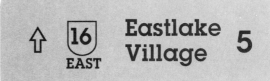

⬆ [16] EAST — Eastlake Village **5**

There are seven towns altogether on the shores of Snake Lake. They're connected by bridges and winding highways.

---

from *United We Solve*

Discrete math, optimization, maps.

Cluster: Networks

Here is the schedule for the #101 bus:

Whittle County Buses
#101 Circle Route
The schedule for each hour is the same from 8:00 am until 7:00 pm:

clockwise	counter-clockwise
Placer 8:05	Monroe 8:00
Monroe 8:20	Placer 8:15
Flint 8:35	Tyler 8:30
Tyler 8:50	Flint 8:45
Placer 9:05	Monroe 9:00

Help your group plan your route! Begin and end in Placer.

Here is the schedule for the #35 bus:

Whittle County Buses
#35 Monroe-Tyler
The schedule for each hour is the same from 8:00 am until 7:00 pm:

northbound	southbound
Tyler 8:10	Monroe 8:40
Whittle 8:25	Whittle 8:55
Monroe 8:40	Tyler 9:10

Your group's job is to schedule a bus trip that will take you to all six towns in Whittle County.

Here is a diagram of the inter-city buses in Whittle County.

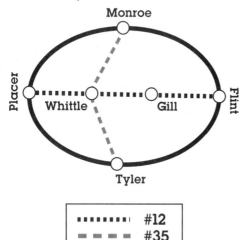

··········	#12
– – – –	#35
▬▬▬▬	#101

You can start as early as 8:30, and you need to finish as soon as possible.

from *United We Solve*

Here is the schedule for the #12 bus:

Whittle County Buses
#12 Placer-Flint
The schedule for each hour is the same from 8:00 am until 7:00 pm:

eastbound	westbound
Placer 8:00	Flint 8:30
Whittle 8:10	Gill 8:40
Gill 8:20	Whittle 8:50
Flint 8:30	Placer 9:00

You must spend at least 17 minutes in each town, so you will have to get off the bus in each town and catch another bus.

Discrete math, optimization. Multiple solutions. Challenging.   **Cluster: Networks**

Spatial

When we were growing up, K–12 mathematics education focused on speed and accuracy with numerical calculations. Then we hit high-school geometry. Suddenly we faced spatial reasoning—mixed with the notion of proof—in a single deadly concoction. Things have changed some-what; geometry is becoming more inferential, proof is rightly seeping into other areas of mathematics, and, from an early age, students are getting experience with geometry, measurement, and spatial reasoning.

There is a feeling of fun that clings to spatial lessons. Students often complain (or gleefully exclaim) that they "aren't doing math."

Let's keep the fun, and also recognize the math. Spatial reasoning permeates important, legitimate mathematics. It's vital to anyone who continues in a math-based field such as physics, business, or medicine. And it can be learned. Before it was a major part of the curriculum, many students passed or failed geometry on the basis of their spatial experience outside of class. If you played with Tinkertoys® a lot, you understood isosceles right triangles; if you didn't, you had some catching up to do. (Who got to play with Tinkertoys? And who aced geometry? Think about it.) Now a more balanced population is ready to go on to study more mathematics.

While other problems in the book may have a spatial dimension (e.g., all of the problems in the *Inaccessible Distances* cluster, pages 178–182), the clusters of problems in this category are primarily spatial.

Arrange the Blocks

Materials: colored blocks, possibly a mat

Math: geometry, direction, logic, spatial visualization

This is a large and diverse cluster, but in every problem, groups arrange a set of colored blocks based on clues. Three of these problems—*Eternal Flame*, *Colored Stairs*, and *Edgy*—are based on logic and geometrical terminology (e.g., the red block shares a face with the blue block). The rest have visual rather than linguistic clues. You may want to review some terminology with your students. If they have forgotten or never learned the difference between edges and faces, for example, some of the problems may seem like "tricks."

Some teachers have students draw their structures on isometric dot paper.

Point of View 1 through 4

Each clue is a perspective drawing of a structure from a different vantage point. Some blocks are invisible on an individual clue. The group is supposed to build the structure.

When we tested these problems, in some groups (if they have enough blocks), each student built what he or she could see. Then the students compared their structures to see the common features, and built a common structure. Other groups naturally tended to build a common structure from the beginning. You may want to suggest one technique or the other, or be silent on the matter, observe the work, and ask about it during debriefing.

When the structure is built, each student is supposed to indicate where—relative to the structure—his or her clue's "picture" was taken. They can do this many ways, including placing their clues on the table around the structure, with the position of the clue indicating the position of the "camera."

Many groups find that it's useful to build their structures on a paper "mat" or even something more durable such as a plastic lid. They can then rotate the structure on the table in order to see it from different angles.

Eternal Flame

This problem has only word clues, although students still build the structure. While not simple, this one yields to a little logic. An "answer" hint for the teacher: though there is only one block on the first level, there are *four* on the second.

- Which clue helped you the most?

Arrange Six

Each student gets a view of the six blocks, but each can see only four. Some blocks are hidden behind others. Each clue tells which direction—North, South, East, or West—the person is from the blocks.

Lost Labels

Here students get the views but don't know which side each view is from. Their task is to build the object and then label it.

Views 1 and 2

In these problems, each group member gets a "drafting" view—with dotted lines for hidden edges. The group builds the structure.

Things don't always go well the first time. No matter what order they try these two problems in, people seem to think the first one they do is much harder than the second. This is an advertisement for practice and persistence.

Many students (and adults) are unfamiliar with the conventions about dashed and solid lines and are initially perplexed by the whole experience—but then, with one problem under their belts they think the next one really interesting and fun and accessible to fifth graders. Also, you may want to indulge in a little instruction about the "seams" rule (card △) and the dashed-line convention.

- How would you explain to somebody what dotted lines mean? How about solid lines?

- How many drawings do you need in order to know what a structure looks like? (There is no right answer. It depends on the structure.)

Colored Stairs (word clues)

This is subtle but rewarding. At first, it doesn't look as if there is enough information to solve the puzzle. We think there are two solutions, each a reflection of the other.

- (During) What do you know about the numbers and colors of the blocks?

Edgy (word clues)

In this problem, students are asked to build at least two different solutions and to write one more clue that will make the solution unique.

Be sure to read the extra clues. They suggest a way for groups to check each other's solutions. If you want to omit this, remove the relevant clue.

Each person has a different drawing of the same structure. Work together to build it with blocks. Then figure out where the "point of view" of *this* clue is. Place this card there.

Each person has a different drawing of the same structure. Work together to build it with blocks. Then figure out where the "point of view" of *this* clue is. Place this card there.

102

Each person has a different drawing of the same structure. Work together to build it with blocks. Then figure out where the "point of view" of *this* clue is. Place this card there.

Each person has a different drawing of the same structure. Work together to build it with blocks. Then figure out where the "point of view" of *this* clue is. Place this card there.

from *United We Solve*

3-D geometry. Starter.

Cluster: Arrange the Blocks

Each person has a different drawing of the same structure. Work together to build it with blocks. Then figure out where the "point of view" of *this* clue is. Place this card there.

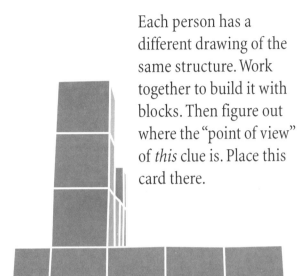

Each person has a different drawing of the same structure. Work together to build it with blocks. Then figure out where the "point of view" of *this* clue is. Place this card there.

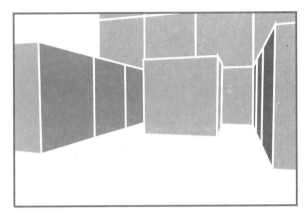

read student solutions at www.eeps.com

students! send your solutions to answers@eeps.com

Each person has a different drawing of the same structure. Work together to build it with blocks. Then figure out where the "point of view" of *this* clue is.

Place this card there.

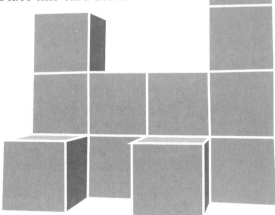

Each person has a different drawing of the same structure. Work together to build it with blocks. Then figure out where the "point of view" of *this* clue is. Place this card there.

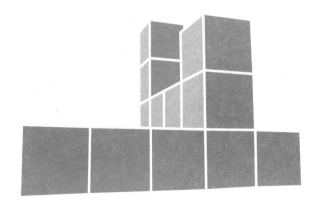

103

read student solutions at www.eeps.com

students! send your solutions to answers@eeps.com

from *United We Solve*

copyright © 1996 by eeps media

3-D geometry.

Cluster: Arrange the Blocks

▲ Point of View 3

Each person has a different drawing of the same structure. Work together to build it with blocks. Then figure out where the "point of view" of *this* clue is. Place this card there.

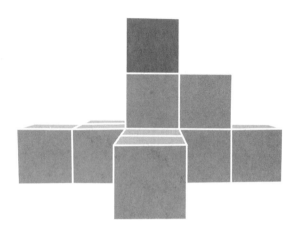

▼ Point of View 3

Each person has a different drawing of the same structure. Work together to build it with blocks. Then figure out where the "point of view" of *this* clue is. Place this card there.

◄ Point of View 3

Each person has a different drawing of the same structure. Work together to build it with blocks. Then figure out where the "point of view" of *this* clue is. Place this card there.

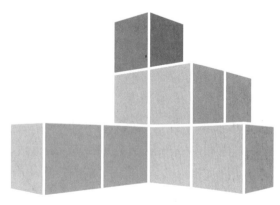

► Point of View 3

Each person has a different drawing of the same structure. Work together to build it with blocks. Then figure out where the "point of view" of *this* clue is. Place this card there.

from *United We Solve*

copyright © 1996 by eeps media

3-D geometry.

Cluster: Arrange the Blocks

▲ Point of View 4

Each person has a different drawing of the same structure. Work together to build it with blocks. Then figure out where the "point of view" of *this* clue is. Place this card there.

▼ Point of View 4

Each person has a different drawing of the same structure. Work together to build it with blocks. Then figure out where the "point of view" of *this* clue is. Place this card there.

◄ Point of View 4

Each person has a different drawing of the same structure. Work together to build it with blocks. Then figure out where the "point of view" of *this* clue is. Place this card there.

► Point of View 4

Each person has a different drawing of the same structure. Work together to build it with blocks. Then figure out where the "point of view" of *this* clue is. Place this card there.

from *United We Solve*

copyright © 1996 by eeps media

3-D geometry. POW. Challenging.

Cluster: Arrange the Blocks

▲ Eternal Flame

There are nine blocks altogether, including three reds.

One of the two green blocks touches five other blocks: two blues, two yellows, and a red.

Build It!

◀ Eternal Flame

Each blue block shares two faces with yellow blocks.

Build It!

106

○ Eternal Flame

Two of the red blocks touch only other reds.

Build It!

▼ Eternal Flame

Only one block touches the table, and it's green.

This structure may not stand up if it's only partly built.

Build It!

▶ Eternal Flame

Each yellow block shares two faces with blue blocks.

Build It!

△ Eternal Flame

The highest block is on the sixth level up from the table.

Build It!

---

from *United We Solve*

copyright © 1996 by eeps media

3-D geometry. Word clues.

Cluster: Arrange the Blocks

Arrange Six

You are at the North side of the table, looking South. That means that East is on your left and West is on your right.

Here is what you can see (some blocks may be hidden):

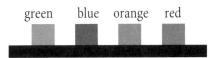

Help your group arrange the six blocks so that they are consistent with all of the clues.

Arrange Six

You are at the East side of the table, looking West. That means that South is on your left and North is on your right.

Here is what you can see (some blocks may be hidden):

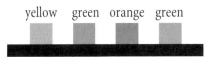

Help your group arrange the six blocks so that they are consistent with all of the clues.

Arrange Six

You are at the West side of the table, looking East. That means that North is on your left and South is on your right.

Here is what you can see (some blocks may be hidden):

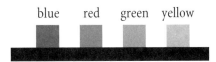

Help your group arrange the six blocks so that they are consistent with all of the clues.

Arrange Six

You are at the South side of the table, looking North. That means that West is on your left and East is on your right.

Here is what you can see (some blocks may be hidden):

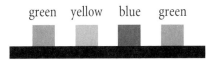

Help your group arrange the six blocks so that they are consistent with all of the clues.

from *United We Solve*

3-D geometry, compass directions.

Cluster: Arrange the Blocks

The Lost Labels

Lobelia and Ravi made a cube of eight blocks and drew a picture of each face. Then they lost the labels.

Help your group build the cube and decide on the right label for this picture.

The Lost Labels

Ravi and Lobelia made a cube of eight blocks and drew a picture of each face. Then they lost the labels.

Help your group build the cube and decide on the right label for this picture.

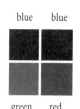

The Lost Labels

Help your group build this cube and decide on the right label for this picture.

Labels might be words such as *North*, *Side*, *Top*, or *West* (or others…)

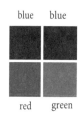

The Lost Labels

Lobelia and Ravi made a cube of eight blocks and drew a picture of each face. Then they lost the labels.

Help your group build the cube and decide on the right label for this picture.

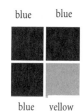

The Lost Labels

Ravi and Lobelia made a cube of eight blocks and drew a picture of each face. Then they lost the labels.

Help your group build the cube and decide on the right label for this picture.

The Lost Labels

Help your group members build the cube and decide on the right label for their clues.

This clue tells you that there are four blue blocks, two reds, one yellow, and one green.

from *United We Solve*

3-D geometry.

Cluster: Arrange the Blocks

Views 1

A

View from the South.

The solid lines are edges that don't touch other blocks.

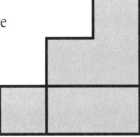

Views 1

▼

This is a top view.

Work with your group to build the structure.

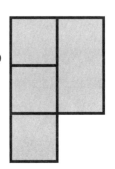

Views 1

◄

View from the North. Dashed lines show hidden edges.

Views 1

►

View from the West.

Lines between blocks don't appear—only edges in the structure.

Views 1

○

View from the East. Dashed lines show hidden edges.

There are eight blocks in this structure.

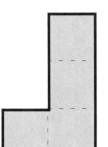

Views 1

△

Remember: the "seams" between the blocks don't show. So a side view of these two blocks:

Looks like this:

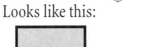

Not like this:

East   North   West   South

from *United We Solve*

copyright © 1996 by eeps media

3-D geometry, hidden edges, compass directions.

Cluster: Arrange the Blocks

Views 2

View from the
East. A solid line
shows an edge
that doesn't touch
other edges.

Views 2

▼

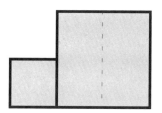

View from the West. A dashed
line shows a hidden edge.

◄ Views 2

Work with your group
to build this structure:

This is a view from the
South. A dashed line
shows a hidden edge.

► Views 2

Work with your group to
build this structure:

This is a view from the
North. A dashed line
shows a hidden edge.

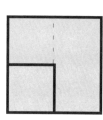

110

○ Views 2

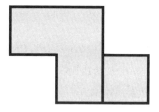

This is a top view. North is at the right.

△ Views 2

Remember: the "seams" between the
blocks don't show. So a side view of these
two blocks:

Looks like this: Not like this:

East   North   West   South

from *United We Solve*

copyright © 1996 by eeps media

3-D geometry, hidden edges, compass directions.

Cluster: Arrange the Blocks

▲ Colored Stairs

The twelve blocks form a stairway two blocks wide and three blocks tall.

Build It!

▼ Colored Stairs

There are four colors in this problem, including yellow.

Each red block has a blue block on top of it.

Build It!

◄ Colored Stairs

The arrangement of the blue blocks is identical to the green, but reversed.

The four blocks on the middle level are all different colors.

Build It!

► Colored Stairs

Each block touches blocks of the same color only at corners (not on edges or faces).

Build It!

○ Colored Stairs

There are four green blocks, including some on every level.

Build It!

△ Colored Stairs

Each yellow block has a green block on top of it, but not all green blocks have yellow blocks beneath them.

Build It!

from *United We Solve*

3-D geometry, symmetry. Multiple solutions. Word clues.

Cluster: Arrange the Blocks

111

▲ Edgy

Each of the two orange blocks shares an edge with the red block.

No two blocks in this puzzle share a face.

Build it—and make a new clue!

▼ Edgy

The two orange blocks share an edge.

At no place in this puzzle do more than two blocks share the same edge.

Build it—and make a new clue!

◄ Edgy

Each of the two green blocks shares an edge with one of the orange blocks.

Your job, as a group, is to find at least two ways to build this puzzle and to write one more clue that will make only one solution possible.

► Edgy

The blue block shares two edges: one with each green block.

Altogether there are two oranges, two greens, one red, and one blue block in this puzzle.

Build it—and make a new clue!

○ Edgy

Some solutions to this puzzle have all of the blocks sitting flat on the table. They're really two-dimensional solutions.

Extension: Can you and your group find three-dimensional solutions?

△ Edgy

Extension: When you have made your extra clue, trade with another group and test their clue to see if it really determines a solution. They will test yours as well.

3-D geometry. Multiple solutions. Write a new clue. Word clues.   **Cluster: Arrange the Blocks**

Maps

Materials: scissors, blank map mats for each problem

Math: spatial reasoning, logic, map skills, geography

Each of these problems features a blank map; the group's clues help them place the labels on the maps correctly. After they do a problem or two, you can invite students to make up problems about some other part of the world, for example, U. S. states. (Many Californians, for example, can't tell Vermont from New Hampshire.) We have also included a blank map of Canada on page 187 (with labels for the provinces and territories) so you can make up a problem about that country.

The clues for all these problems involve which countries border on which, and which countries you pass through on imaginary journeys. Students can check their answers with an atlas or a globe.

General Questions

- Which clue was a good one to start with?
- Which country was the hardest to figure out? Why?
- Can you definitely place any countries yet?
- Can you eliminate any possibilities?

Central America

We would hope that more students would know which countries are which without the clues, but they do not. This is a chance to learn—and a chance for a native of one of these countries to shine with some prior knowledge.

Eastern Europe, Central Asia

These two problems focus on countries of the former Soviet Union. Who among us can reliably pick out Uzbekistan or Moldova? This is a chance for students to learn some of the countries that weren't around when we were kids. Both are harder than Central America.

- Can you find the Danube River on a map?
- If K2 is the second-highest mountain, what's the highest mountain?

West Africa

If this is too easy, use the label for Ghana and white out the "giveaway" label. But we found it too hard without that extra clue. It is embarrassing for us supposedly geographically-literate teachers that we recognize so few countries—and these have been around for longer than those former Soviets! Quick: where's Burkina Faso?

- Can you point to Mount Nimba on the map?

▲ Central America

All of the countries in Central America have two coastlines except for El Salvador and Belize.

Colombia has two coasts, too, though it's in South America.

▼ Central America

Guatemala borders on Mexico, Honduras, El Salvador, and Belize.

El Salvador's capital city is San Salvador.

If you drove the Pan-American Highway to Mexico from Costa Rica, you would travel through four other countries in between.

◄ Central America

If you take the Pan-American Highway from San Salvador (capital city of El Salvador) to the city of Managua, you have to cross two borders: the first as you enter Honduras, and the second as you leave it.

San Jose is the capital of Costa Rica.

► Central America

Managua is the capital city of Nicaragua.

Originally, Colombia and Panama were both part of "Gran Colombia." Panama split off from Colombia in 1903.

Belize is the only country in Central America that the Pan-American Highway does not go through.

114

Guatemala

Nicaragua

Costa Rica

Honduras

Panama

Mexico

Colombia

Belize

El Salvador

from *United We Solve*

copyright © 1996 by eeps media

Logic, geography.

Cluster: Maps

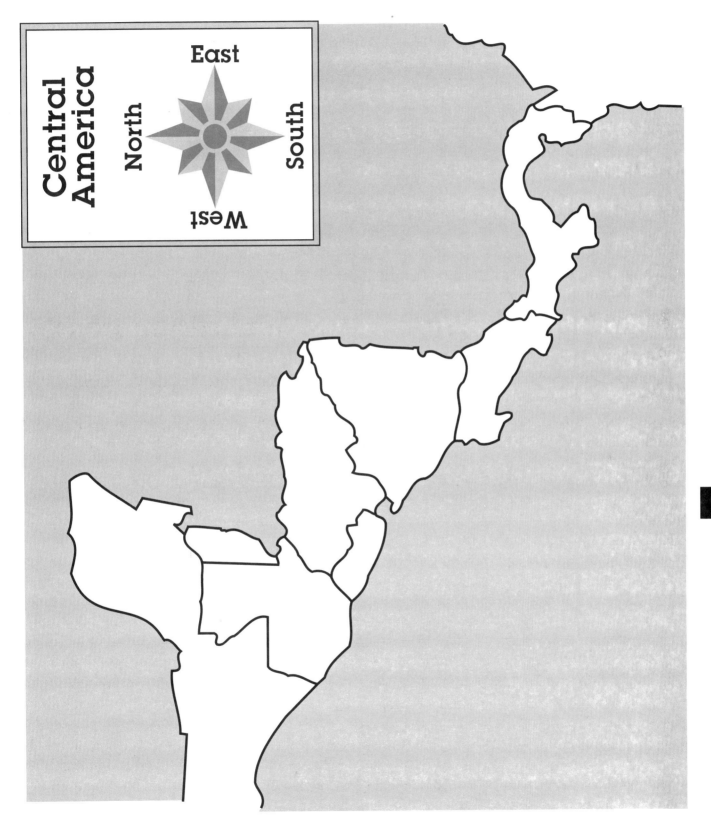

Central America

East
North
South
West

Eastern Europe

Russia has two parts: the big part that extends eastward into Asia, and the little part that's between Poland and Lithuania. Kaliningrad—formerly known as Königsberg—is in the little part, famous to mathematicians for its seven bridges.

Belarus, Moldova, Slovakia, Hungary, and the Czech Republic have no coastline.

Budapest is the capital of Hungary. It sits on the Danube far upstream from where that river empties into the Black Sea.

Eastern Europe

Estonia, Latvia, and Lithuania are known as the Baltic Republics because they're on the Baltic Sea, which is west of those three countries and north of Poland.

Istanbul, the largest city in Turkey, is located on the Bosporus, a narrow strait connecting the Black Sea eventually to the Mediterranean. The northwestern bit of Turkey is in Europe; the rest is in Asia.

Bratislava is the capital of Slovakia.

Eastern Europe

The Carpathian Mountains occupy much of Slovakia. They are also in southern Poland and they extend eastward into Ukraine and then south into Romania, where they meet the Transylvanian Alps.

Moldova is a small country between Romania and Ukraine.

If you traveled by road from Bucharest, Romania to Prague, in the Czech Republic, you'd probably go through Budapest and Bratislava, in that order.

Eastern Europe

The Danube River forms much of the border between Romania and Bulgaria.

Estonia is the northernmost Baltic Republic.

The Crimea is currently part of Ukraine, though Russia seems to want it. It is a peninsula extending into the Black Sea.

There used to be a country called Czechoslovakia. It was composed of the Czech Republic in the the west and Slovakia in the east.

Czech Republic	Slovakia	Estonia	Latvia	Lithuania
Russia	Poland	Belarus	Ukraine	Hungary
Romania	Bulgaria	Turkey	Black Sea	Moldova

from *United We Solve*

Logic, geography.

Cluster: Maps

116

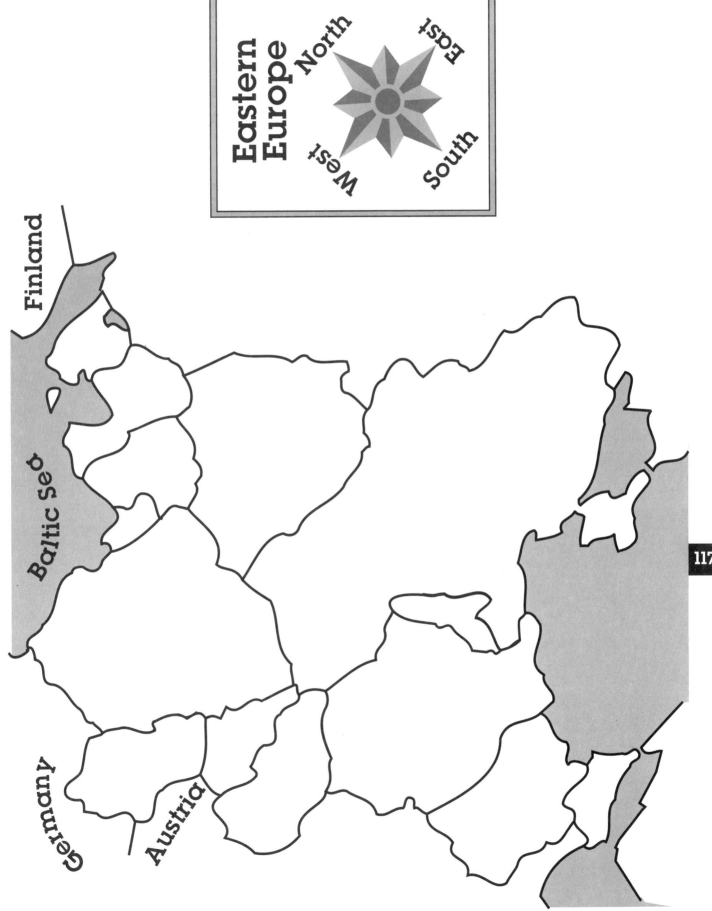

Eastern
Europe

North

East

West

South

Finland

Baltic Sea

Germany

Austria

Central Asia

Mongolia borders on only two countries: China to the south, and Russia to the north.

Jammu and Kashmir is a region made up of parts of northern India and northern Pakistan.

Afghanistan shares a very short border with China.

"*Stan*" means "country."

Central Asia

Azerbaijan, Kazakhstan, Iran, Russia, and Turkmenistan all have shores on the Caspian Sea.

K2, the second-highest mountain in the world, is 8,611 meters (28,250 ft.) high. It sits between Pakistan and China.

The desert east of the Caspian Sea makes up most of Uzbekistan and Turkmenistan.

Central Asia

Baku, the capital city of Azerbaijan, is on the west shore of the Caspian Sea.

Iran and Afghanistan are Turkmenistan's southern neighbors.

If you could walk due north over such mountainous terrain, you could start in Pakistan and travel through Afghanistan, Tajikistan, Kyrgyzstan, Tajikistan again, Uzbekistan, and Kazakhstan to get to Russia.

Central Asia

The Aral Sea sits on the border between Kazakhstan and Uzbekistan.

A road across the Khyber Pass connects Afghanistan and its capital, Kabul, to Islamabad, in Pakistan.

Kazakhstan, Uzbekistan, Turkmenistan, Tajikistan, Azerbaijan, Russia, and Kyrgyzstan all used to be part of the USSR.

Turkmenistan	Uzbekistan	Kyrgyzstan	Kazakhstan	Tajikistan
India	Pakistan	Afghanistan	Aral Sea	Caspian Sea
Azerbaijan	Iran	Russia	China	Mongolia

from *United We Solve*

copyright © 1996 by eeps media

Logic, geography.

Cluster: Maps

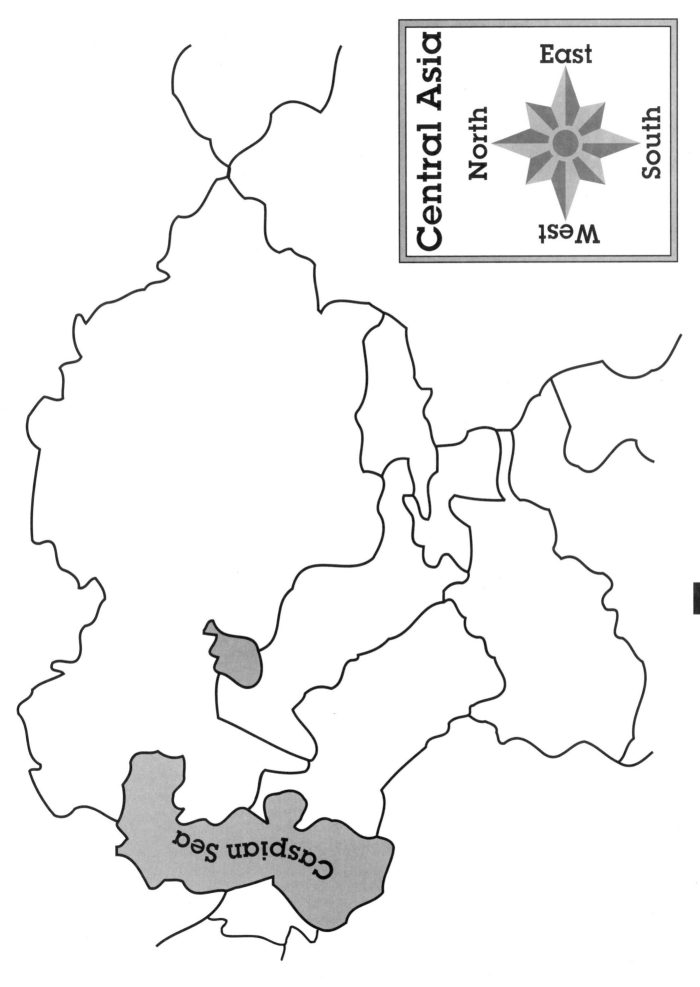

Central Asia

East

North

South

West

Caspian Sea

119

West Africa

Mali, Burkina Faso, and Niger have no coastline.

Guinea-Bissau is between Senegal and Guinea.

The Atlas Mountains stretch westward from Algeria into Morocco, but they end there; they do not extend farther south into Western Sahara.

West Africa

Mount Nimba is right near the place where Liberia, Cote d'Ivoire (also called Ivory Coast), and Guinea meet.

To get from Western Sahara to Mali, you could go southeast through Mauritania (though it would be hot and sandy).

West Africa

Burkina Faso borders on Mali, Niger, Ghana, Togo, Cote d'Ivoire, and Benin. Gambia borders only on Senegal.

The Niger River starts in Guinea, then flows through Mali and Niger before it enters Nigeria, where it flows into the sea. At one point it forms the border between Benin and Niger.

West Africa

There is a road from Sierra Leone that runs eastward through Guinea, by Mount Nimba, and on into Abidjan, the capital of Cote d'Ivoire.

Nigeria shares borders with Cameroon, Niger, Benin, and Chad, though Chad is not in this problem.

Benin	Burkina Faso	Guinea-Bissau	Niger	Nigeria
Senegal	Mauritania	Morocco	Algeria	Mali
Togo	Cote d'Ivoire	Liberia	Cameroon	Ghana
Sierra Leone	Gambia	Guinea	Western Sahara	

from *United We Solve*

copyright © 1996 by eeps media

Logic, geography.

Cluster: Maps

West Africa

North

West

East

South

Ghana

121

Polygons

Materials: scratch paper, pencils, rulers, calculators, protractors

Math: geometry, spatial visualization, scale, proportion

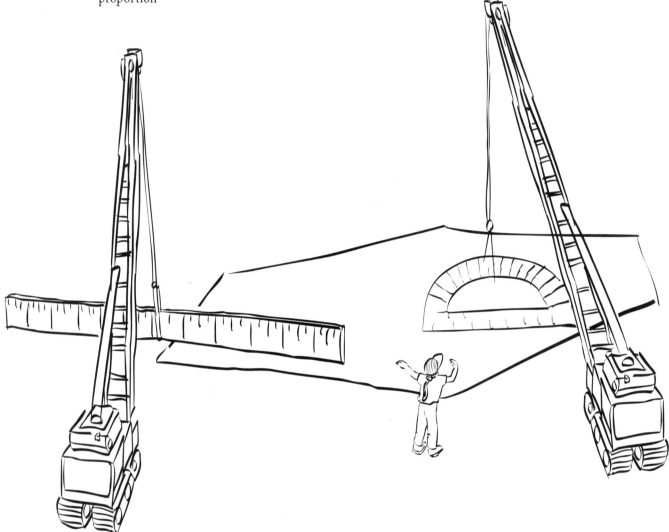

Polygons 1 through 5

In these problems, the group must construct an accurate full-sized or scale drawing of a polygon. The individual clues help the group figure out its shape and size based on properties such as area and perimeter. They get harder as the problem number gets higher.

All problems assume that students can compute the area and perimeter of a rectangle. Beginning in *Polygon 2*, students may need to compute the area of a triangle.

In *Polygon 5*, the figure is a square.

Note: it may look as if we are expecting students to know the Pythagorean theorem. They may use it if they wish, but the intent is that they *measure* the parts of the triangles they cannot compute. For example, if they need the area of an equilateral triangle of side 4.5 cm, they can construct it (perhaps by trial and error), measure its height, and use that in the area formula.

- What do you know so far?

- What was the best clue to start with?

- What was the most important discovery you and your group made?

▲ Polygon 1

All of the angles in this polygon are right angles.

Work with your group to make an accurate drawing of this polygon.

◄ Polygon 1

The perimeter of this polygon is 32 cm.

Work with your group to make an accurate drawing of this polygon.

○ Polygon 1

Hint: One way to figure out this polygon is to look at the area and try to decide what numbers might multiply to give that amount. This could be a problem if the sides weren't whole numbers of centimeters, but in this case they are.

▼ Polygon 1

This polygon is a quadrilateral: it has four sides.

Work with your group to make an accurate drawing of this polygon.

► Polygon 1

This polygon's area is 48 square centimeters.

Work with your group to make an accurate drawing of this polygon.

123

△ Polygon 1

Hint: One way to figure out this polygon is to make a table of possible values and keep changing them until things work out right.

from *United We Solve*

copyright © 1996 by eeps media

Geometry, measurement, area, perimeter, right angles. Drawing (1:1).   **Cluster: Polygons**

▲ Polygon 2

All the sides of this polygon have the same length.

Work with your group to make an accurate drawing of this polygon. Then figure out its area.

▼ Polygon 2

This polygon is a quadrilateral: it has four sides.

Work with your group to make an accurate drawing of this polygon. Then figure out its area.

◄ Polygon 2

The perimeter of this polygon is 18 cm.

Work with your group to make an accurate drawing of this polygon. Then figure out its area.

► Polygon 2

One of the diagonals of this polygon has the same length as one of its sides.

Work with your group to make an accurate drawing of this polygon. Then figure out its area.

○ Polygon 2

Hint: There are many ways to find the area of the polygon. One way is to divide it into triangles and then add the areas of those figures.

△ Polygon 2

One of the diagonals of this polygon is quite a bit longer than the other. If you draw it carefully, it should be about 7.8 cm long.

from *United We Solve*

Geometry, measurement, area, perimeter, diagonals. Drawing (1:1).   **Cluster: Polygons**

Polygon 3

This polygon is a parallelogram. That means that opposite sides are parallel to one another.

Work with your group to make an accurate drawing of this polygon.

Polygon 3

This quadrilateral has an area of 20 square centimeters.

Work with your group to make an accurate drawing of this polygon.

Polygon 3

Two opposite sides of this polygon are each 5 cm long.

Work with your group to make an accurate drawing of this polygon.

Polygon 3

The perimeter of this polygon is 24 cm.

Work with your group to make an accurate drawing of this polygon.

Polygon 3

The area of a parallelogram is its base times its height, where the height is the perpendicular distance between the base and its opposite side.

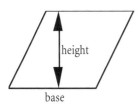

Polygon 3

Any side of a parallelogram can be its base.

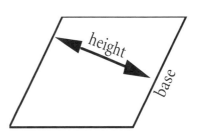

from *United We Solve*

copyright © 1996 by eeps media

Geometry, measurement, area, perimeter, parallelograms. Drawing (1:1).   Cluster: Polygons

Polygon 4

This polygon is a hexagon, and all its sides are the same length.

This polygon fits on a letter-sized piece of paper, but you have to plan carefully.

Help your group make an accurate, full-sized drawing of this polygon.

Polygon 4

This polygon has two lines of mirror symmetry and two right angles—though they may not be next to each other.

Help your group make an accurate, full-sized drawing of this polygon.

Polygon 4

Your group will need paper, pencil, and a centimeter ruler. And possibly a protractor.

Four of the angles inside this polygon measure 135°.

Help your group make an accurate, full-sized drawing of this polygon.

Polygon 4

Your group will need paper, pencil, a centimeter ruler, and possibly a protractor.

The perimeter of this polygon is 72 cm.

Help your group make an accurate, full-sized drawing of this polygon.

Polygon 4

A square with an area of 144 cm^2 will fit snugly into each of the right angles of this figure.

Help your group make an accurate, full-sized drawing of this polygon.

Polygon 4

A rectangle about 12 cm by 17 cm will fit snugly into this figure.

Help your group make an accurate, full-sized drawing of this polygon.

from *United We Solve*

copyright © 1996 by eeps media

Geometry, measurement, angles, perimeter, right angles, symmetry. Drawing (1:1).   Cluster: Polygons

▲ Polygon 5

Your polygon has an area of 18 square centimeters.

Work with your group to make a labeled, full-sized drawing of your polygon.

▼ Polygon 5

The longest line segment that will fit inside your polygon is 6 centimeters long.

You and your group will need paper, pencil, and a ruler (and maybe a calculator) to draw your polygon.

◄ Polygon 5

Each side of your polygon has the same length. Each angle is the same, too.

In order to draw your polygon, you need to figure out how many sides it has.

► Polygon 5

Your polygon has a perimeter of about 17 centimeters.

Guess and check might be a good strategy for figuring out how many sides your polygon has.

○ Polygon 5

It's a little under 22 millimeters from the center of the polygon to the closest point on a side.

Work with your group to make a labeled, full-sized drawing of your polygon.

△ Polygon 5

Your polygon has fewer than eight sides.

Work with your group to make a labeled, full-sized drawing of your polygon.

Extension: Did you find more than one polygon that fits these clues?

from *United We Solve*

Geometry, measurement, area, perimeter, diagonals. Drawing (1:1).   **Cluster: Polygons**

Pyramid Schemes

Materials: card stock or paper, scissors, tape, pencils, rulers, calculators, compasses.
Note: index cards work for the card stock, as do used manila folders.

For *Third of a Cube*, you need at least 10 cm on the short side of an index card, so that means that 5-by-8 (inches) is the smallest US size that will work for that problem.

Other pyramids work with 3-by-5; the cones work better with paper.

Math: geometry in three dimensions, spatial visualization, surface area and volume, proportion

Each problem has three steps: first, you make a shape as an individual. Second, you work with the group to assemble the 3-D figure (pyramids, or, in one case, a cone) with your shape as a face. Finally, you work together to determine the surface area and volume of your figure. Clues give the volume formulas; we assume students know how to find the areas of triangles and squares.

Lower-grades note: if you don't want your students to work out the surface areas and volumes, but just make the figures, use the versions of the first two with asterisks (✻) on the ends of their names. They do not ask for the calculations, only the constructions.

Accuracy note: In determining the volume of some of these pyramids, middle-grades students will probably not be able to do the Pythagorean gyrations necessary to get the answer exactly. Here, we can simply look for a measurement, probing to see whether the student measures the height (correctly) perpendicular to the base or (incorrectly) along one of the convenient edges.

You can verify volumes with rice and a graduated cylinder.

A good extension question for any of these would be, "How would we make one twice as big?" (probing whether they're thinking twice the volume or twice the linear size) or "What would the volume be if we made each triangle 20 cm on a side?" (or whatever is appropriate to the problem).

Weird Juice Box (two versions)

Your students have probably seen these and sucked ice-pops out of them. Even so, it's a little funny-looking. It's interesting to see a tetrahedron made of four congruent triangles that is *not* regular. If students get stuck, focus them on the hint in clue 1: "The base of your triangle will be attached along the base of one other triangle." This will help them avoid the tendency to make a tall, pointy pyramid.

- Is there any other way to make a 3-D figure with these pieces? (You could make a pointy square pyramid if you leave the base open.)

- How did you measure the height of this pyramid for the volume calculation?

Third of a Cube (two versions)

This requires careful measurement. You might suggest that they use the corners of the index cards for the right angles they need. It helps if they remember *isosceles* and *right angle*. If they make the pyramids carefully, three of them fit together into a cube, demonstrating the formula for volume.

For this problem, they should be able to get the volume exactly (one-third of 1000 cm³), because one of the edges is perpendicular to the base.

- Can you fit *any* three identical pyramids together into a cube? …into some kind of box?

Octahedron

Students need to know *vertex* and *equilateral triangle*.

The trick to finding the volume (hinted at in a clue) is to see that an octahedron is two square pyramids stuck base-to-base. They can calculate the area of the square base and measure the height of the pyramid with the ruler. Double the volume of the pyramid to get the octahedron's volume.

Extension: Give each group a loop of string about four meters (two or so armspans) long. Ask them to work together to make the edges of an octahedron. It is possible to do so without doubling any of the edges. They will need several people to hold the vertices.

Make a Cone

Students will need compasses or some other circle-making tool or technique.

You can't make the 20cm diameter circle out of a card, so use paper or card stock.

- Why do you suppose the formula for the volume of a cone is the same as the formula for a pyramid?

About Nets

The problems in this cluster ask students to put together 3-D objects by taping polygons together. Many other activities take a different route to their polyhedra: they ask the students to make *nets* and then fold the nets to make the solids.

Since they're folded, nets use less tape, and can make stronger structures. However, inventing a net requires that you visualize the folding as well as the object. You can't move the faces independently.

You might consider, therefore, using one of these activities (or a similar one that you invent) as a preliminary for making nets. Let the students make the pyramid (or whatever) then *ask them to cut it apart (along the taped edges, at first) so that the result is a single sheet of connected shapes lying flat.* That sheet will be a net for the pyramid.

Of course, there are different ways to cut up a pyramid. There are different nets that all create the same solid. For example, here are two different nets for a pyramid similar to the one in *Third of a Cube*:

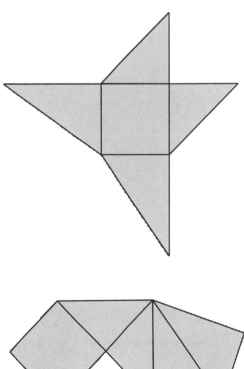

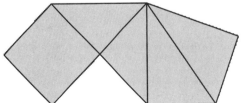

Weird Juice Box

Make an isosceles triangle with a base of 5 cm and a height of 6 cm.

Next, work with your group to assemble your pieces into a single polyhedron.

Then work with your group to measure its volume and surface area.

Hint: The base of your triangle will be attached along the base of one other triangle.

Some juice containers have this shape.

Weird Juice Box

Make an isosceles triangle with a base of 5 cm and a height of 6 cm.

Next, work with your group to assemble your pieces into a single polyhedron. It will be a tetrahedron, but not a regular tetrahedron.

Then work with your group to measure its volume and surface area.

Your group will need cards (or cardboard), scissors, rulers, and tape.

Weird Juice Box

Make an isosceles triangle with a base of 5 cm and a height of 6 cm.

Next, work with your group to assemble your pieces into a pyramid with a triangular base.

Then work with your group to measure its volume and surface area.

You will need a ruler, a pencil, paper (or index cards), and scissors to make your triangle.

Hint: You may not be able to calculate the height of your pyramid, but you can measure it.

Weird Juice Box

Make an isosceles triangle with a base of 5 cm and a height of 6 cm.

Then work with your group to assemble your pieces into a single polyhedron.

Hint: Your pieces will probably look about the same.

Formula for the volume of a pyramid:

$$V = Bh/3$$

where B is the area of the base (in your case, a triangle) and h is the height of the pyramid.

from *United We Solve*

Measurement, geometry, isosceles triangles, volume, surface area.   **Cluster: Pyramids**

⬆ Weird Juice Box✳

Make an isosceles triangle with a base of 5 cm and a height of 6 cm.

Then work with your group to assemble your pieces into a single polyhedron.

Hint: The base of your triangle will be attached along the base of one other triangle.

Some juice containers have this shape.

The *height* of a triangle is probably not the length of a side. It's the shortest (right-angle) distance from the base to the far corner of the triangle.

⬇ Weird Juice Box✳

Make an isosceles triangle with a base of 5 cm and a height of 6 cm.

Then work with your group to assemble your pieces into a single polyhedron. It will be a tetrahedron, but not a regular tetrahedron.

Your group will need cards (or cardboard), scissors, tape, and rulers.

◄ Weird Juice Box✳

Make an isosceles triangle with a base of 5 cm and a height of 6 cm.

Then work with your group to assemble your pieces into a pyramid with a triangular base.

A pyramid with a triangular base is also called a *tetrahedron*. *Tetra* means "four," and a tetrahedron has four faces (counting the base).

► Weird Juice Box✳

Make an isosceles triangle with a base of 5 cm and a height of 6 cm.

Then work with your group to assemble your pieces into a single polyhedron.

An *isosceles* triangle has two sides the same. The base is the other side.

Hint: Your pieces will probably look about the same.

from *United We Solve*

Measurement, geometry, isosceles triangles.

Cluster: Pyramids

Third of a Cube

Make two identical isosceles right triangles. The "like" sides in the triangles should each be 10 cm long, and they should meet in a right angle. The hypotenuse—the long side—of the triangles should end up about 14.1 cm long.

Next, work with your group to assemble your pieces into a single pyramid.

Then work with your group to determine its volume and surface area.

Hint: Your two triangles should be connected along one of their 10-cm edges.

Third of a Cube

Make a square 10 cm on a side. Use card stock or a big index card.

Next, work with your group to assemble your pieces into a single polyhedron. It will have five faces.

Assemble your polyhedron with tape. Or, if you want, you can make your triangle with tabs on the edges for gluing.

Then work with your group to determine its volume and surface area.

When you're done, work with two other groups to see if you can fit your three pyramids together into a cube.

Third of a Cube

Make a right triangle. One of the sides on the right angle will be 10 cm long. The other will be 14.1 cm long. (Measure carefully and be sure the right angle is really a right angle!) The hypotenuse—the long side, opposite the right angle—will be about 17.3 cm long.

Next, work with your group to assemble your pieces into a pyramid with a square base.

Then work with your group to determine its volume and surface area.

Your group will need rulers, pencils, tape, paper (or large index cards), and scissors.

132

Third of a Cube

Make a right triangle. One of the sides on the right angle will be 10 cm long. The other will be 14.1 cm long. (Measure carefully and be sure the right angle is really a right angle!) The hypotenuse—the long side, opposite the right angle—will be about 17.3 cm long.

Then work with your group to assemble your pieces into a single polyhedron.

Formula for the volume of a pyramid:

$$V = Bh/3$$

where B is the area of the base and h is the height of the pyramid.

from *United We Solve*

Measurement, geometry, isosceles and right triangles, volume, surface area.   Cluster: Pyramids

▲ Third of a Cube✳

Make two identical isosceles right triangles. The "like" sides in the triangles should each be 10 cm long, and they should meet in a right angle. The hypotenuse—the long side—of the triangles should end up about 14.1 cm long.

Then work with your group to assemble your pieces into a single pyramid.

Hint: Your two triangles should be connected along one of their 10-cm edges.

▼ Third of a Cube✳

Make a square 10 cm on a side. Use card stock or a big index card.

Then work with your group to assemble your pieces into a single polyhedron. It will have five faces.

Assemble your polyhedron with tape. Or, if you want, you can make your triangle with tabs on the edges for gluing.

When you're done, work with two other groups to see if you can fit your three pyramids together into a cube.

◀ Third of a Cube✳

Make a right triangle. One of the sides on the right angle will be 10 cm long. The other will be 14.1 cm long. (Measure carefully and be sure the right angle is really a right angle!) The hypotenuse—the long side, opposite the right angle—will be about 17.3 cm long.

Then work with your group to assemble your pieces into a pyramid with a square base.

Your group will need rulers, pencils, tape, paper (or large index cards), and scissors.

▶ Third of a Cube✳

Make a right triangle. One of the sides on the right angle will be 10 cm long. The other will be 14.1 cm long. (Measure carefully and be sure the right angle is really a right angle!) The hypotenuse—the long side, opposite the right angle—will be about 17.3 cm long.

Then work with your group to assemble your pieces into a single polyhedron.

When you're done, work with two other groups to see if you can fit your three pyramids together into a cube.

from *United We Solve*

Measurement, geometry, isosceles and right triangles.   **Cluster: Pyramids**

Octahedron

Make two equilateral triangles 8 cm on a side. Then work with your group to assemble your pieces into an octahedron.

To measure its volume, think of it as two pyramids.

Hint: Four faces will meet at every vertex of your polyhedron.

You will need tape to assemble your octahedron. Or, if you want, you can make your triangles with tabs on the edges for gluing.

Octahedron

Make two equilateral triangles 8 cm on a side. Then work with your group to assemble your pieces into an octahedron. Your octahedron will be a regular solid with eight identical faces.

Next, work with your group to measure its volume and surface area.

When you're done (or while you're calculating), look at the outside. It is made up of eight triangles. But if you look at it another way, you can see that it is also made of three squares. Color the three squares in three different colors.

Octahedron

Make two equilateral triangles 8 cm on a side. Then work with your group to assemble your pieces into an octahedron. It will look like two square pyramids stuck together.

Then work with your group to measure its volume and surface area.

Your group will need will need rulers, pencils, paper (or card stock), a calculator, three markers of different colors, and scissors to finish this task.

Extension: What do you think would be the volume of an octahedron 16 cm on a side?

Octahedron

Make two equilateral triangles 8 cm on a side. Then work with your group to assemble your pieces into a single octahedron.

Hint: You may not be able to calculate the height of your triangles or your polyhedron, but you can measure it.

Formula for the volume of a pyramid:

$$V = Bh/3$$

where B is the area of the base and h is the height of the pyramid.

from *United We Solve*

copyright © 1996 by eeps media

Measurement, geometry, equilateral triangles, volume, surface area.   **Cluster: Pyramids**

Make a Cone

Carefully measure and cut out a circle with a diameter of 20 cm. This will be called the "big circle."

Then give it to the person who is supposed to cut it in half. Next, work with your group to assemble a cone.

Finally, work with your group to determine its volume and surface area.

The formula for the area of a circle is

$$A = \pi R^2$$

Where R is the radius of the circle.

Make a Cone

Carefully measure and cut out a circle with a diameter of 10 cm. This will be called the "little circle."

Then work with your group to assemble a cone. Taping the circular part will be the hardest.

Finally, work with your group to determine the cone's volume and surface area.

Hint: Finding the surface area may seem hard at first, but think about the pieces the cone was made of.

Make a Cone

When the person making the big circle is done, carefully cut it in half along the diameter before you start making the cone.

Then work with your group to assemble a cone.

Finally, work with your group to determine its volume and surface area.

Your group will need rulers, tape, pencils, paper (or card stock), a calculator, something to make circles (such as a compass), and scissors to complete your task.

Make a Cone

Work with your group to assemble one of the big semicircles and the little circle into a cone. Measure its volume and surface area.

Formula for the volume of a cone:

$$V = Bh/3$$

where B is the area of the base (in this case, a circle) and h is the height of the cone. This is the same formula as the one for the volume of a pyramid.

Be sure your group can explain why the big semicircle wrapped all the way around the little circle. It should have fit exactly.

135

from *United We Solve*

Measurement, geometry, circles, volume, surface area.

Cluster: Pyramids

Directions

Materials: rulers, calculators, scratch paper, protractors

Math: scale, direction, angle, bearing, constraints

In this cluster, students use the clues to figure out where something is. Some problems use bearings in degrees (0° is north, 90° is east, and so forth, up to 360°), but we do not expect students to use trigonometry. Instead, they should make scale drawings. Groups need to figure out an appropriate scale. Unlike the *Networks* cluster, this one is geometrical, not discrete.

You may want to suggest that some groups make scratch-paper manipulatives to move around as they solve these problems.

In these problems, students need to realize that if a ship is 25 km from Bora Bora, that means that the ship is somewhere on a *circle* of radius 25 km, centered on Bora Bora. If students have never seen this, some of them will probably figure it out working in groups. Then, in debriefing, you can have the students explain it. Imagine not having to do that yourself!

If you have access to computers, some of these problems can be modeled using dynamic geometry software such as *The Geometer's Sketchpad* from Key Curriculum Press.

Jake and Emily

A good starter. Instead of arbitrary position, this takes place on a grid—with city blocks. So distances are in blocks, and all directions are north, south, east, or west.

- If you walk from one corner of a block to the opposite corner of the same block, how many blocks of walking is that? (It's two in the problem, but see what they think.)

- What is it about Group 4's map that makes their solution clear?

Amityville Area

From here through *Urak's Treasure*, the problems use continuous rather than city-block distances. All distances are straight.

If students make a scale drawing, and use the "circle" technique on clue 3, "Amityville is 12 kilometers from Eastwick," they will see that that circle intersects the southeast ray from Bodega Bay (Clue 2: "Eastwick is directly southeast of Bodega Bay.") in two places. That generates two rather different solutions.

On the other hand, less careful students (and adults) have made the Bodega Bay ray *tangent* to that circle. They didn't measure or draw to scale. That yields one solution, and often they seem satisfied with it. Depending on the experience of your students, you may be satisfied, too; they will still have figured out a lot of directional mathematics.

Be alert for groups that see both solutions—and don't let them share their solutions first.

- How did you deal with the clue, "The distance from Stepford to Eastwick is the same as the distance from Stepford to Amityville?" (They may not be ready for perpendicular bisectors; guess and check is fine. On the other hand, some students may begin to get the idea of a locus here, which is excellent preparation. Watch for it.)

- How do you know it's two solutions and not just one?

Hawaii Flight 1

If you have circular compasses, break them out! We begin using bearings in a real-life air navigation problem. In this one, the direction to Honolulu is easy, but the distance is not. This is a good candidate for a scale drawing.

- Which was harder to figure out, direction or distance?
- How did you figure out the direction?
- How did you figure out the distance?

These VORs—the radio beacons—are abstract ideas for most students. If any parent is a private pilot, you can ask for an expired map and let students see the VORs on them; they're at the centers of large compass-rose circles. If no parents have old air charts, you can buy such a map for a few dollars at many small airports—or tell them you're a teacher and they may give you a few expired ones. They're very colorful and *full* of where-will-I-ever-have-to-use-this mathematics.

Hawaii Flight 2

This is harder than *Hawaii Flight 1*, and requires more careful drawing. The group has to find the closest airport to your location, and you have only bearings from radio beacons to guide you. The group also must determine the distance and bearing to the airport.

- Compare with other groups. Do you all agree on which airport to fly to?
- When—or if—you made your scale drawing, what point did you start with? How did you decide on it?
- One clue says, "Don't confuse the airport with the VOR!" What does that mean?

Urak's Treasure

A more fanciful problem, this one gives you clues for where to dig for a buried treasure. There are two solutions (based on where two circles intersect), though clue △ helps decide where to dig first. The task asks for a scale map showing where to dig. Some students make their map entirely in zwatloos, rather than converting to traditional units.

- How far is 100 zwatloos? More than the length of this room? Longer than the soccer field? As far as from here to downtown?
- What's an obelisk?
- Compare your map with another group's. How closely do you agree?
- If you were actually there looking for the treasure, what would you do to decide where to dig?

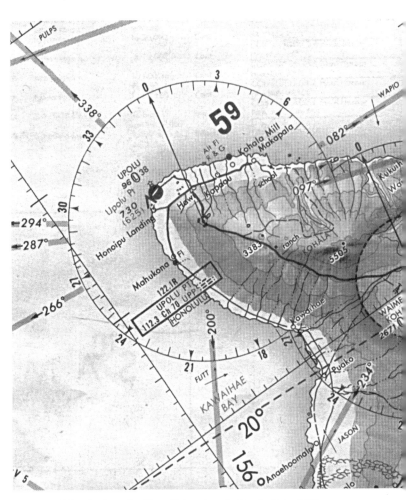

Part of the air chart for Hawaii showing the Upolu Point VOR. It's at the middle of the big circle. The airport is the dark circle up and to the left. Groups do not need this to solve the problem.

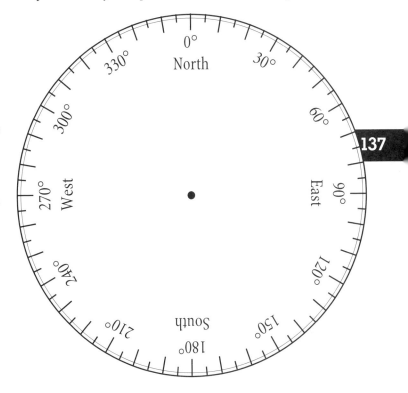

Students can use these to get their bearings.

Jake & Emily

To get from his house to school, Jake walks four blocks north and one block west.

How do you get from school to the grocery store?

Jake & Emily

To get to Emily's house from his house, Jake walks one block north and three blocks west.

After school, Jake and Emily decide to walk to the grocery store. Give them directions!

Jake & Emily

To get home from the hardware store, Emily walks one block east and two blocks south.

How do you get from school to the grocery store?

Jake & Emily

To get to the hardware store from the grocery store, you have to go five blocks west.

After school, Jake and Emily decide to walk to the grocery store. Give them directions!

138

Jake & Emily

A walk from school to the hardware store is four blocks.

Hint: One way to solve this problem is by drawing a map on a piece of grid paper. If you're careful, you can do it without the grid.

Jake & Emily

Emily has to walk five blocks to school.

The streets in Jake and Emily's town are laid out in a grid. There are no curved streets or streets that cut across on a diagonal.

from *United We Solve*

copyright © 1996 by eeps media

Compass directions, grid geometry. Starter.

Cluster: Directions

▲ Amityville Area

Bodega Bay is 15 km north of Amityville.

Your job, with your group, is to make a map showing where all the towns are in relation to one another.

▼ Amityville Area

Eastwick is directly southeast of Bodega Bay, and Amityville is due west of Stepford.

The map you and your group make should be drawn to scale.

◄ Amityville Area

Amityville is 12 kilometers from Eastwick.

There may be more than one way to draw your map.

► Amityville Area

The distance from Stepford to Eastwick is the same as the distance from Stepford to Amityville.

All distances in this problem are measured in a straight line. Don't worry about curvy roads.

○ Amityville Area

Stepford and Amityville are the southernmost towns in the area.

Your job, with your group, is to make a scale map showing all the towns in the Amityville area (there are four).

△ Amityville Area

Bodega Bay is the northernmost town in the Amityville area. The real Bodega Bay, in Northern California, is the site of Alfred Hitchcock's *The Birds*.

Your job, with your group, is to make a scale map showing all the towns in the Amityville area (there are four).

from *United We Solve*

Compass directions, geometry. Scale drawing.

Cluster: Directions

Hawaii Flight 1

It's cloudy down below and you have to find your way to Honolulu International Airport (HNL).

Your instruments tell you that you are due north of the Lanai VOR — bearing 0°.

You'll probably need a ruler and a protractor.

Hawaii Flight 1

Your instruments tell you that you are due east of the Molokai VOR. That's a bearing of 90°. In bearings, 0° is north.

A bearing of 142° is kind of southeast—in fact, 52° south of east (since 142 – 90 = 52).

A VOR is a radio transmitter. Think of it as a point on a map.

Hawaii Flight 1

It's 44 nautical miles (abbreviated NM) from the Molokai VOR to Honolulu International Airport, and 25 NM from the Molokai VOR to the Lanai VOR. (1 NM = about 1.85 km or about 6080 ft.)

What direction do you fly to get to the Honolulu airport? How far away is it?

Hawaii Flight 1

Honolulu International is almost due west (that is, bearing 270°) of the Molokai VOR. The Lanai VOR is at a bearing of 142° from the Molokai VOR.

You and your group need to figure out how far away the airport is and what direction you need to fly to get there.

Hawaii Flight 1

You are 20 NM from the Lanai VOR.

Kamakou, the highest point on Molokai, is northeast of you. Molokai and Lanai are two of the Hawaiian islands.

Hint: You may need to make a scale drawing to figure this out. The Molokai VOR is a good starting place.

Hawaii Flight 1

Your instruments tell you your bearing from the VOR. VOR stands for Visual Omni Range. It's a radio transmitter.

Hint: You can figure out where you are by making a triangle using bearings from two VORs. That's what pilots (and their computers) do.

from *United We Solve*

Compass bearings, geometry, multiple questions. Realistic context.

Cluster: Directions

⋀ Hawaii Flight 2

You're having engine trouble. How far is it to the nearest airport?

The Maui VOR is located at the Kahului Airport.

Your plane is at a bearing of 028° from the Upolu Point VOR.

⋁ Hawaii Flight 2

You're having engine trouble. Which airport is nearest—Hana, Upolu, or Kahului?

The Hana airport, on Maui, is 24 NM from the Maui VOR at a bearing of 095°.

Your plane is at a bearing of 100° from the Maui VOR.

◄ Hawaii Flight 2

Upolu Airport is 4 NM (nautical miles; 1 NM is about 1.85 km or about 6080 ft) from the Upolu Point VOR, at a bearing of 325°. Don't confuse the airport with the VOR!

In bearings, 0° is due north, 90° is east, 180° is south, and 270° is west. You'll need a ruler and a protractor (or an air chart).

► Hawaii Flight 2

You're flying over the ocean near the Hawaiian Islands. What direction (bearing) should you fly to get to the nearest airport?

The Upolu Point VOR, on the "big island" of Hawaii, is 53 NM from the Maui VOR at a bearing of 130°.

A VOR is a radio beacon.

○ Hawaii Flight 2

Hint: You may need to make a scale drawing to figure this out. It also might help if you've already done *Hawaii Flight 1*.

A bearing of 130° is between east (90°) and south (180°), so it's more or less southeast. To be more accurate, measure the direction with a protractor: it should be 40° south of due east.

△ Hawaii Flight 2

VOR stands for Visual Omni Range. It's a kind of radio beacon pilots can use to find their way. Your instruments tell you your bearing from the VOR.

Hint: You can figure out where you are by making a triangle using your bearings from the two VORs. That's what pilots (and their computers) do.

---

from *United We Solve*

Compass bearings, geometry, multiple questions. Realistic context. POW.   **Cluster: Directions**

Urak's Treasure

Legend has it that the Enormous Treasure of King Urak the Rich was buried in the ancient city of Urakopolis, 300 zwatloos from the Lost Obelisk of Urak.

Unfortunately, the obelisk is lost. So is the rest of Urakopolis except for a stone which is definitely the northeast cornerstone of the Great Library of Urak.

Urak's Treasure

An inscription recovered from the Branch Library at Urak Minor tells you that the Enormous Treasure of King Urak the Rich was buried 200 zwatloos from the southwest cornerstone of the Great Library of Urak in Urakopolis.

Where should you dig? Make a scale map showing your group's decision.

Urak's Treasure

The Great Library of Urak was a square 100 zwatloos on a side. One zwatloo, by the way, was the height of King Urak the Rich himself. And we have his skeleton. He was 182 cm tall.

Where should you dig? Make a scale map showing your group's decision.

Urak's Treasure

Although the Lost Obelisk of Urak is lost, plans for the ancient city of Urakopolis show that the obelisk was built exactly 250 zwatloos due south of the center of the Great Library of Urak.

Where should you dig? Make a map, drawn to scale, showing your group's decision.

Urak's Treasure

Hint: There is more than one possible place to dig, given your information. On your map, you will want to show as many sites as you can that are consistent with the clues.

Urak's Treasure

One of the possible digging sites is within 100 zwatloos of the Great Library of Urak.

Hint: That's the least likely site for burying an Enormous Treasure, because it is so close to a public place.

from *United We Solve*

Directions, geometry, proportion. Scale drawing. Multiple solutions. POW. **Cluster: Directions**

Round and Round

Materials: scratch paper, pencils, calculators, possibly compasses

Math: geometry, circles

As with "Rates," most traditional circle problems don't have four pieces of information. So here is a set of problems in which different circles interact in interesting ways. These circle problems use the same kind of thinking you need later on in mathematics but do not require more than $C = \pi D$ and common sense.

Wayne's Wheel

How thick is Wayne's wheel? Students may have difficulty with the vocabulary of wheels; they may never have thought about measuring the *hub* of a wheel. Students also have to be—or become—clear about the difference between *circumference* and *diameter*. Drawings on the cards attempt to help. They will need to use the circumference formula (provided on clue ➤) to find the diameter given the circumference. You should read clue ○, also.

- Where did you start in this problem?
- How did you calculate the radius of the hub once you knew its circumference?

Lillian's Island

Given the length of a route across and around the island, find its radius. You can use algebra if you want on this problem, but you don't have to. Clue △ gives a suggestion: figure the length of the route if the island's radius were 1 km. It will be less than the 12 km you need. So scale it up proportionally.

- How did your group represent Lillian's route? Did you draw it? Make a table? What?
- How did your group figure out the radius?
- How accurate do you have to be to be done?

Track and Field

The task is to make a scale drawing of a track and field layout given the length of the inside of the track. There are many solutions. One of the most straightforward is to make each "curved" part 100 m long. In that case, students must calculate its radius in order to make the scale drawing. The circumference formula is given in clue ▼, but they will have to invert it (to find the radius) and be sure not to double or halve the relevant circumference (because there are two pieces).

If there were a four-point rubric, the typical—and common—"2" response would be simply to say that the curved pieces are each 100m long and to make a drawing that was not a scale drawing. In that case, you might ask:

- What's the scale of your drawing?
- How do you know that this curved part is 100m long?

Strapping Ladd

Part of the answer: the curved parts together make a circle. If you don't believe it, look at the case of two or four tanks. And the straight parts are each two radii (or one diameter). Students should get this by common sense if they draw a good picture. Seventh graders can do this, especially with the hints.

Double Ferris

This problem is for eighth grade and above.

When will Dwayne and Ursula be together at the top again? Each is on a different Ferris wheel. They move at different speeds. But proportions connect them.

There are at least two routes to the solution: you can do a lot of calculator work, figuring circumferences in meters and speeds in meters per second; or you can use ratios and realize that (for example) since the Gigante has 5/4 the radius of the Majestic, it has 5/4 of the circumference. Knowing it goes 3/2 as fast, you know it goes the same distance in 2/3 the time. And 2/3 times 5/4 is 5/6 the time, or 5/6 of 11 seconds for the Gigante to go around.

Wayne's Wheel

Wayne's wheel goes around four times when it rolls ten meters.

How thick is Wayne's wheel?

Wayne's Wheel

The circumference of the hub of Wayne's wheel is the same as the diameter of the wheel itself.

How thick is Wayne's wheel?

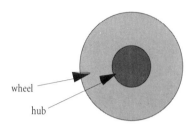

wheel

hub

Wayne's Wheel

The thickness of Wayne's wheel is the same as the radius of the hub.

How thick is Wayne's wheel?

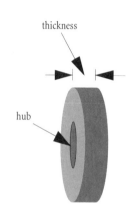

thickness

hub

Wayne's Wheel

Two useful formulas about circles:

$$C = \pi d \text{ and } d = 2r$$

where C = circumference, d = diameter, and r = radius.

How thick is Wayne's wheel?

Wayne's Wheel

Common sense, but easy to forget: When a wheel rolls around once—if it doesn't slip—the distance it travels is the *circumference* of the wheel.

How thick is Wayne's wheel?

Wayne's Wheel

Wayne's wheel is thicker than a bicycle wheel but thinner than one from a car.

How thick is Wayne's wheel?

from *United We Solve*

copyright © 1996 by eeps media

Geometry, measurement, circles.

Cluster: Round and Round

Lillian's Island

Lillian lives at the center of a circular island. What's its diameter?

When she has her clams, she takes the trail home and makes clam chowder for lunch.

After dinner, she comes straight home.

Lillian's Island

Every day Lillian walks 12 kilometers. What's the diameter of Lillian's Island?

After lunch (and a nap) Lillian packs a picnic dinner and hikes through the jungle to North Beach for her afternoon swim.

Lillian's Island

When Lillian leaves her hut in the morning, she walks directly to South Beach for her morning swim.

After her afternoon swim, she hikes along the beach to West Beach, where she watches the sunset and eats dinner.

What's the diameter of her island?

Lillian's Island

Lillian's island is lush but flat. All the jungle trails are straight, and there's a splendid beach that curves all the way around the island.

After her morning swim, Lillian walks along the beach (counterclockwise) to East Beach, where she digs clams.

Lillian's Island

In the course of her day, Lillian walks the radius of her island four times.

It will help to draw a map of the island and trace Lillian's daily route on it.

The radius of the island is half the diameter. For this problem, you may use $\pi = 3.14$.

Lillian's Island

In the course of a day, Lillian does not walk the entire circumference of her island.

The circumference of a circle is related to the radius by

$$C = 2\pi R$$

Hint: If the radius were 1 kilometer, how far would Lillian walk each day?

from United We Solve

Geometry, circles, proportion

Cluster: Round and Round

Track and Field

Taylor Middle School is putting in an oval track. It will have two parallel straight parts and two curved parts. Each curved part will be a semicircle.

These are semicircles.

Track and Field

The new Taylor Middle School track will enclose the playing field, which is 55 meters wide. There must be some space between the playing field and the track.

The circumference of a circle is related to the radius by the formula:

$$C = 2\pi R$$

You may use $\pi = 3.14$ for this problem.

Track and Field

The inside edge of the new Taylor Middle School track must have a perimeter of exactly 400 meters. (If you run at the outside of the track, it will be longer.)

Your job, as a group, is to make a scale drawing of the track and the field that meets all of the specifications.

Track and Field

The new Taylor Middle School track will enclose the playing field, which is 100 meters long.

Your job, as a group, is to make a scale drawing of the track and the field that meets all of the specifications.

Track and Field

Hint: In making your scale drawing, choose a convenient scale. To do that, think about the biggest dimension in your drawing. How big is the track?

Common sense, but easy to forget: The length of a semicircle is half the circumference of a circle with the same radius.

Track and Field

As you make your plan, you will have some flexibility in the dimensions of the track. That's OK—just be sure you meet all the specifications: the shape of the track, its circumference, and that it completely encloses the field.

Geometry, circles, proportion. Scale drawing. Multiple solutions. POW.   **Cluster: Round and Round**

▲ Strapping Ladd

Larry Ladd has to strap three oxygen tanks together into a cluster. How much strap does he need?

Work with your group to figure it out. Don't forget to draw a picture!

▼ Strapping Ladd

Larry Ladd decides to make a cluster of tanks. He wants to use as little strapping as possible, so he packs the tanks together as tightly as they will go.

How much strap does he need?

◄ Strapping Ladd

Each oxygen tank is a long cylinder 24 cm in diameter.

The circumference of a circle is related to the diameter by the formula:

$$C = \pi D$$

You may use $\pi = 3.14$ for this problem.

► Strapping Ladd

Larry Ladd decides to use two straps: one near the top and one near the bottom. How much strap does he need?

Larry will need 10 cm extra on each strap for the buckle.

○ Strapping Ladd

Hint: This can be tricky. When you draw it, you'll see that there are curved parts of the strap and straight parts. Figure the curved parts separately from the straight.

Another Hint: For the curved parts, see if you can figure out the length of all them together if you can't figure them out separately.

△ Strapping Ladd

Extension: What if Larry had strapped one tank? What about 2? What would be the shortest strap for four? How would you arrange the tanks then? Five? Six? Seven?

from *United We Solve*

Geometry, circles, proportion, tangents, packing. POW.

Cluster: Round and Round

⋏ Double Ferris

Dwayne and Ursula went to the county fair and rode two Ferris wheels that were side-by-side.

The seats on the Majestic travel two-thirds as fast as those on the Gigante.

⋎ Double Ferris

The radius of the Majestic wheel is four meters.

Just as the ride began, and the last people were being loaded, Dwayne and Ursula noticed that they were both at the top of their respective Ferris wheels.

◄ Double Ferris

The radius of the Gigante Ferris wheel is five meters.

Dwayne rode the Majestic; Ursula rode on the Gigante.

How long will it be before Dwayne and Ursula are both at the top of their wheels at the same time again?

► Double Ferris

Just because a seat moves faster doesn't mean that the Ferris wheel will get around more quickly. Remember: the Gigante is bigger than the Majestic.

It takes eleven seconds for the Majestic to go all the way around.

○ Double Ferris

If one circle has twice the radius of another, its circumference is twice as big, too.

The circumference of a circle is related to the radius by the formula:

$$C = 2\pi R$$

You may use $\pi = 3.14$ for this problem.

△ Double Ferris

Hint: In this problem, it will be useful to figure out how long it takes the Gigante to go all the way around. It is quicker than the Majestic.

How long will it be before Dwayne and Ursula are both at the top of their wheels at the same time again?

from *United We Solve*

Geometry, circles, frequency, time, proportion. POW.

Cluster: Round and Round

Proportion

Proportion has many faces. We use proportion in geometry and measurement when we use similarity and make scale drawings; we use proportion in statistics and probability when we sample and calculate expected value. But this category of problems is more prosaic. It's about the bread and butter of the middle-grades curriculum: fractions, decimals, and percents.

There's no way around it: Computing and reasoning with rational numbers are essential skills. That doesn't mean, however, that students need to spend the middle years with worksheets adding fractions with unlike denominators. The problems you'll find here emphasize fractions and especially percents. Using the calculator to find percentages uses decimals as well.

There are three directions a simple numerical proportion problem can go:

Find the Proportion. Taylor Middle has 1240 students. 186 walk to school. What percentage walk? (15%)

Find the Little Number. Taylor Middle has 1240 students. 15% walk to school. How many walk? (186)

Find the Big Number. At Taylor Middle School, 15% walk to school. That's 186 students. How many attend Taylor altogether? (1240)

In general, the latter type—Find the Big Number—is harder, both conceptually and computationally. It's one of the few situations where it's appropriate to divide by a fraction or a percent. Because individuals can be confused by this kind of problem, it is especially appropriate for groups.

A simple proportion problem won't have enough separate clues for this format, so none of these problems are of the simple type. They either require more parts to make up the whole (45% ride their bikes, 15% walk, 32% take the bus, and the rest use Pogo sticks. How many is that?) or there are linked proportions (Sally has sixty; Bob has half as many as Sally; Tamara has two-thirds as many as Bob; Enrique has one-fifth as many as Tamara...), or some other context or complication that adds more necessary information.

It All Adds Up

Math: fractions, decimals, percents, proportion

Materials: scratch paper, pencils, manipulatives, calculators

Description

This cluster is all about fractions and percents and how they add up to one. The solutions to the problems all have to do with knowing what proportion some quantity is of the whole.

Four A

Four kids are sharing a pizza, but the pieces are not the same size. What fraction does each kid get? Clues give proportions among the pieces, and, of course, the four fractions add to one.

If students are having trouble, suggest they use manipulatives.

- How did your group figure out the fractions?

- When you finished, how did you know you were right?

Favorite Pets/Favorite Plants

These two are related "survey" questions. "Pets" is easier. You try to figure out what fraction of kids prefer a certain pet, given clues about the others. "Plants" is the "backwards" version; you try to figure out how many people were in the survey. Groups can use manipulatives to great advantage here, as the numbers are not as large as they will find a little later on.

Autumn Leaves

How many leaves did Trevor the Tree have at the beginning of the month? This problem introduces an odd property of percent problems: They often have more than one answer.

Here's what we mean by that: One kind of percent calculation says, 76 is 8% of something; what's the something? We divide by a percentage: $76 \div .08 = 950$. But a percentage implies that it has been rounded to the nearest percent. After all, what's 8% of 951? 76 is 7.99% of 951; we'd clearly report that as 8%. Similarly, if someone told us that 15% of the school's 680 students ate tuna sandwiches, we wouldn't be surprised if it was only 100 (14.7%) instead of 102.

- Do you think that's a reasonable number for leaves on a tree?

- What's the biggest number we got as an answer? The smallest? Do you think all the numbers in between are OK? How can a problem like this have more than one answer?

Sandwiches 8/Sandwiches 7

NOTE: "8" is easier than "7;" again, 8 is forward (How many kids had sandwiches?) and 7 is its backward twin (Given various information about sandwiches, how many kids were there?). All the percentages and fractions in these two problems are exact, so the rounding issues in *Autumn Leaves* and others do not apply. That is, the numbers are cooked to work out nicely, even though the percentages and fractions appear ugly.

In Sandwiches 7, the easy way to do it involves noticing that if 3/8 of all kids bring their lunches and 2/3 of those have sandwiches, then the fraction of all kids who brought sandwiches is

$$(3/8) \times (2/3) = (2/8) = (1/4) .$$

This may be too sophisticated for some, but it is a genuine use of proportion and fractions. A group may come to use it where an individual might not.

Both of these problems ask the groups to make a visual display.

- What are the different kinds of displays we made?

- Do any have more information than others?

- What do you think is the most important information?

Spikeys & Blesboks

This problem is a lot like *Sandwiches 7* except that percentages are rounded to the nearest percent. As in *Autumn Leaves*, that yields multiple solutions. So there are really two parts: using logic and percent-reasoning to get an answer, and then figuring out what other answers are possible. As clue ○ suggests, this is a chance for the group to split up the calculations and let everyone get into the act.

Four A

Arlo and Angel Fauré, the twins, get identical pieces.

What fraction of the pizza does each person get?

Four A

Alice's piece is three times the size of her brother Andy's.

What fraction of the pizza does each person get?

Four A

Andy's piece is half the size of his brother Arlo's.

What fraction of the pizza does each person get?

Four A

The four Faurés are sharing one pizza four ways. But the pieces are not all the same size.

What fraction of the pizza does each person get?

Four A

Alice's piece is one and one-half times the size of Angel's.

What fraction of the pizza does each person get?

Four A

Together, Alice and Andy have as much as the twins.

What fraction of the pizza does each person get?

151

Fractions, pizza. Starter.

Cluster: All Adds Up

Favorite Pets

Fifteen kids answered the favorite pet survey at Pets Galore in the Allendale Mall. The four choices were: turtle, pot-bellied pig, capybara, and cockatiel.

What fraction of the kids preferred pot-bellied pigs?

Favorite Pets

One-third of the kids preferred turtles.

What fraction of the kids preferred pot-bellied pigs?

Favorite Pets

The number of kids who preferred cockatiels was 20% of the number who preferred turtles.

What fraction of the kids preferred pot-bellied pigs?

Favorite Pets

The number of kids who preferred capybaras was 120% of the number who preferred turtles.

What fraction of the kids preferred pot-bellied pigs?

Favorite Pets

Six times as many kids preferred capybaras (the world's largest rodent) as preferred cockatiels.

What fraction of the kids preferred pot-bellied pigs?

Favorite Pets

More than half of the kids preferred a mammal.

What fraction of the kids preferred pot-bellied pigs?

from *United We Solve*

copyright © 1996 by eeps media

Fractions, percents, survey results. Starter.

Cluster: All Adds Up

▲ Favorite Plants

They held a "Favorite House Plants" Survey at Plants Galore in Allendale.

Four people preferred the Split-leaf Philodendron.

How many people were in the survey?

▼ Favorite Plants

The number of people who preferred the African Violet was the same as the number that preferred the Boston Fern.

There were only four choices; each person had to choose only one of the four.

◄ Favorite Plants

One-third of everyone surveyed preferred the most popular plant, the Venus Fly-trap.

How many people were in the survey?

► Favorite Plants

One-fourth of all the people surveyed preferred the Boston Fern.

How many people were in the survey?

○ Favorite Plants

Only half as many preferred the Split-leaf Philodendron as preferred the Venus Fly-trap.

How many people were in the survey?

△ Favorite Plants

Hint: You might use some beans or other manipulatives to represent people in the survey. Then you can use guess and check.

Remember, there were only four choices.

153

Fractions, survey results.

Cluster: All Adds Up

▲ Autumn Leaves

In the first week of November, Trevor lost 65% of his leaves.

How many leaves did Trevor have at the beginning of the month?

▼ Autumn Leaves

Trevor the Tree (he's an oak) had 212 leaves left after three weeks of November.

How many did he start the month with?

There are several possible answers.

◄ Autumn Leaves

In the second week of November, Trevor lost 45% of all the leaves he had at the beginning of that week.

How many leaves did Trevor start with at the beginning of November?

► Autumn Leaves

In the third week of November, Trevor lost 55% of the leaves he had at the beginning of the week.

How many leaves did Trevor have at the beginning of November?

○ Autumn Leaves

Hint: Guess and check is not a terrific strategy for finding one answer, but once you have one, you can use it to find more nearby.

Trevor the Oak Tree started with more than 2,000 leaves.

△ Autumn Leaves

Hint: You can use algebra if you want, though just working backwards will solve this problem for you.

Trevor started with fewer than 3,000 leaves.

from *United We Solve*

Percents. Multiple solutions.

Cluster: All Adds Up

Sandwiches 8

350 eighth graders attended Taylor Middle School last Wednesday.

Figure out how many kids had sandwiches at Taylor Middle School last Wednesday. The display you make with your group should be clear, that is, people should be able to figure out the most important information without getting confused.

Sandwiches 8

3/7 of Taylor's eighth graders bring lunches. The rest buy lunch in the cafeteria.

Figure out how many kids had sandwiches at Taylor Middle School last Wednesday. Then make a visual display of the data.

Sandwiches 8

31% of the cafeteria lunches sold to eighth graders last Wednesday featured sandwiches.

Figure out how many kids had sandwiches at Taylor Middle School last Wednesday. Your visual display might be a single graph or a set of graphs. Don't forget to label it!

Sandwiches 8

72% of the eighth graders who bring lunches have some kind of sandwich in their lunch.

Figure out how many kids had sandwiches at Taylor Middle School last Wednesday. You should be able to get that number from the display you make, but you should be able to figure out other things as well.

Sandwiches 8

Last Wednesday, less than half of Taylor students had sandwiches, but only by a few percent.

Figure out how many kids had sandwiches at Taylor Middle School last Wednesday. Then work with your group to make a visual display that shows as much information clearly as you can.

Sandwiches 8

Last Wednesday at Taylor Middle School, 20 more students bought sandwiches in the cafeteria than brought lunches (from home) without sandwiches.

Figure out how many kids had sandwiches at Taylor Middle School last Wednesday.

from *United We Solve*

Fractions, percents. Group display.

Cluster: All Adds Up

Sandwiches 7

192 seventh graders at Taylor Middle
School had sandwiches last Wednesday.

Figure out how many seventh graders were
at Taylor Middle School last Wednesday.
The display you make with your group
should be clear—that is, people should be
able to figure out the most important
information without getting confused.

Sandwiches 7

3/8 of Taylor's seventh graders bring
lunches. The rest buy lunch in the
cafeteria.

Figure out how many seventh graders were
at Taylor Middle School last Wednesday.
Then make a visual display of the data.

It helps if you've already done the problem
Sandwiches 8. It's easier.

Sandwiches 7

40% of the cafeteria lunches sold to
seventh graders last Wednesday featured
sandwiches.

Figure out how many seventh graders were
at Taylor Middle School last Wednesday.
Your visual display might be a single graph
or a set of graphs. Don't forget to label it!

Sandwiches 7

2/3 of the seventh graders who bring
lunches have some kind of sandwich in
their lunch.

Figure out how many seventh graders were
at Taylor Middle School last Wednesday.
You should be able to get that number from
the display you make, but you should be
able to figure out other things as well.

156

Sandwiches 7

Figure out how many seventh graders
came to Taylor Middle School last
Wednesday. Then work with your group to
make a visual display that shows as much
information as clearly as you can.

Of the seventh graders who did not have
sandwiches, only 25% brought lunches
from home.

Sandwiches 7

Last Wednesday at Taylor Middle School,
twice as many seventh graders bought
sandwiches in the cafeteria as brought
lunches without sandwiches from home.

Figure out how many seventh graders
attended Taylor Middle School last
Wednesday.

from *United We Solve*

Fractions, percents. Group display.

Cluster: All Adds Up

⌃ Spikeys & Blesboks

42% of Hamilton seventh graders wear Spikeys.

How many seventh graders are there at Hamilton?

⌄ Spikeys & Blesboks

37% of Hamilton seventh graders wear Blesboks.

How many seventh graders are there at Hamilton?

◂ Spikeys & Blesboks

All of the percentages in this problem were rounded to the nearest percent. And, by the way, no one wears both Spikeys and Blesboks.

How many seventh graders are there at Hamilton?

▸ Spikeys & Blesboks

55 Hamilton seventh-graders wear some other brand of shoe: neither Spikeys nor Blesboks.

How many seventh graders are there at Hamilton?

○ Spikeys & Blesboks

Hint: There are quite a few solutions to this problem. When you find one, you might try nearby numbers. There's enough calculation that you'll want everyone in your group to help.

△ Spikeys & Blesboks

Hint: What number is 25% of 280? You might think it is 70, but what about 71? Rounded to the nearest percent, it's 25% as well.

How many seventh graders are there at Hamilton?

from *United We Solve*

copyright © 1996 by eeps media

Fractions, percents. Multiple solutions.

Cluster: All Adds Up

Per

Materials: scratch paper, pencils, manipulatives, calculators

Math: number, proportion

These problems involve finding and using "per-unit" quantities and other rates: the price of one slice of apple; the right price per piece of fruit to make a profit of $5; how much frozen juice to buy every two weeks; how many newspapers you need to papier-mâché a giant basketball.

Students are often confused about whether they should multiply or divide when they calculate a per-unit quantity, and they're often confused about what the quantity means once they get it. Help them remember to say the quantity *with units*, and occasionally restate what that means, as in "So you got 12¢ *per slice*; that is , for every slice you use, it costs twelve cents." "Bob traveled 45 *miles per hour*; that is, if he drove for an hour, he'd go 45 miles."

These are related to *Rates* problems; in those, the "per" quantity is always time.

Price of a Slice

How much does one slice of apple cost, given information about the price, weight, and so forth, of apples? It requires fractions and decimals, good practice at eighth grade, but many fifth graders can handle it. The extensions in clue △ are good for the debriefing, or even for a written-up problem. The answer is between 5¢ and 6¢.

- If you were going to charge money for apple slices, what would you charge? How much money would you make or lose?

Fruit Stand

Like *Price of a Slice*, this problem is a pretty straightforward money problem, but it introduces the idea of a profit. Accessible at fifth grade.

Juice Shopping

This problem is more complex, with more context and choices built in. It uses larger numbers, too. There are some questions to think about in clues ○ and △.

- How many drinks of juice do the Trans serve in a week?
- How did you account for the friends on Sunday? How did you account for Saturdays?

Giant Basketball

How many newspapers do you need to papier-mâché a giant basketball? You need to know its surface area, and a clue gives that formula. Groups also need to know how to compute the area of a rectangle. The solution juggles the number of pages in a newspaper, their area, the fact that you need six layers, and the area of the sphere. Because of the formula and the sphere, this is probably a seventh-grade question.

- How did your group keep track of the information?
- How big would a three-meter-diameter sphere be? What would it look like in this room?
- What's the size of a real newspaper?

▲ Price of a Slice

Blaise is going to cut up a large number of apples as part of a snack for all of Taylor Middle School.

A bag of apples weighs 5 kg.

What is the price of a slice?

◄ Price of a Slice

Your group's job is to figure out how much each apple slice will cost.

There are 23 apples in a bag.

What is the price of a slice?

○ Price of a Slice

Hint: You may want a calculator for this problem, though manipulatives should help, too.

You will probably need to figure out some other quantities on the way to the answer. For example, some people calculate the cost of a single apple.

▼ Price of a Slice

Figure out how much a slice of apple will cost. (The school wants to know.)

Apples cost $1.49 per kilogram.

Blaise bought one bag of apples to cut up.

What is the price of a slice?

► Price of a Slice

Your group's job is to figure out how much each apple slice will cost.

Blaise will cut each apple into 6 slices.

What is the price of a slice?

△ Price of a Slice

Extension: Suppose there are 900 students at Taylor and, on the average, each person eats one slice.

How many bags of apples should Blaise buy? How much will it all cost? How long will it take Blaise to cut them up? (Blaise had better get help!)

159

from *United We Solve*

copyright © 1996 by eeps media

Number, fractions, money. Starter.

Cluster: Per

Fruit Stand

Nathan and Oscar decided to sell fruit to make money. They bought a dozen apples for $2.10.

Manipulatives might help you in this problem.

Fruit Stand

There were seven bananas in each bunch.

Oscar and Nathan decided they wanted a single price for a piece of fruit rather than a different price for apples and bananas.

Fruit Stand

Hint: What would happen if they charged 10¢ for each piece of fruit? How much money would they make?

Something extra to think about: What is a reasonable price for a piece of fruit?

160

from *United We Solve*

Number, profit, money. Multiple solutions.

Fruit Stand

Nathan and Oscar decided to sell fruit to make money. But first they had to buy some, so they bought two bunches of bananas for $1.56.

Fruit Stand

Nathan and Oscar want to have $5.00 more after they sell all the fruit than when they started. How much should they charge for a piece of fruit?

In other words, they want a $5.00 *profit*.

Fruit Stand

Hint: The profit they make will be their *income* (the money they get from their customers) minus their *expenses* (the money they had to pay to buy the fruit).

You could even make an equation:

Profit = Income – Expenses.

Cluster: Per

▲ Juice Shopping

The Tran family loves orange juice. Each person drinks between 200 and 300 mL (that's about a cup) a day—and twice that on Saturdays.

The abbreviation mL stands for milliliters. 1000 mL makes one liter, which is a little more than a quart.

◄ Juice Shopping

Each of the Tran children usually invites a friend over for breakfast on Sunday. Their friends like juice just as much as they do.

Then, on Monday, they shop. How many cans of frozen orange juice should they buy to last them for two weeks?

○ Juice Shopping

There are seven days in a week.

Here are some things to think about:

If each person drinks 200–300 mL per day, what number should you use? If you were really shopping, would you buy a little extra?

▼ Juice Shopping

There are six people in the Tran family: the father, Quan; the mother, Vanessa; the kids, Khanh, Luong, and baby Mui (who is already five); and the grandfather, Leonard.

► Juice Shopping

They buy frozen orange juice in 355 mL cans. To make the stuff you drink, you mix that with three cans of water (it makes a total of 1420 mL of juice).

Work with your group to answer the questions.

△ Juice Shopping

Here are some things to think about:

Why does one can of frozen juice make 1420 mL of the stuff that you drink?

Extension: Do the Trans drink a realistic amount of juice? How much orange juice do *you* drink?

161

Number, juice, capacity.

Cluster: Per

▲ Giant Basketball

The surface area of a sphere is given by the formula:

$$A = 4\pi r^2$$

where r is the radius of the sphere. You can use 3.14 for pi (π).

How many newspapers will they need to make the basketball?

◄ Giant Basketball

To make papier-mâché, you use a wire frame and lay goopy strips of newspaper over it, at least six layers thick.

Each sheet of paper in the newspaper is 80 cm wide and 60 cm tall.

○ Giant Basketball

Hint: Don't forget that the formula uses *radius* and you know the *diameter*. Be sure you use the radius of the sphere in the formula!

Be sure you can picture a 3-meter basketball. How big is it? Can a shoe fit inside it? You? Your house?

from *United We Solve*

Geometry, measurement, surface area. POW.

▼ Giant Basketball

They're building a giant papier-mâché basketball for the awards ceremony. They want to make it three meters (that's 300 cm) in diameter and paint it day-glo orange.

You and your group have to figure out how many whole newspapers they need for the papier-mâché.

► Giant Basketball

The local newspaper is 64 pages long, but the pages are printed so that four pages are on each sheet of paper. (Your newspaper is probably like that, too.)

That makes 16 sheets of paper in each edition.

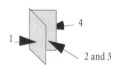

△ Giant Basketball

Extension: A quart of day-glo orange paint says it covers 10 square meters.

How many quarts of paint do they need to paint this basketball?

Cluster: Per

Mixtures

Materials: scratch paper, pencils,
              manipulatives, calculators

Math: proportion, ratios, fractions,
              percents

Simple mixture problems aren't amenable to this format because there are seldom four pieces of information: Anastasia wants a gallon of orange juice and you mix water 3:1 with the frozen stuff. How much of each does she want? It's really only worth two clues.

This collection contains problems that are more complex, so *your students must be able to do simple problems like Anastasia's in order to approach these.* They don't have to be experts, however. Remember that students in a group can solve more difficult problems than they can individually.

Sophisticated, older students may want to use symbolic algebra, but each problem can be solved with common sense, manipulatives, and guess-and-check techniques.

Juice for Fifty

How many cans of frozen orange juice do you need for fifty people? How many pitchers? (Note that there are two questions in this problem.) This is a fairly straightforward problem with numbers that don't get too large. Students will approach it in a number of ways; help them contrast their solutions when you debrief them.

While this uses English measurements, there is enough information for thoroughly metric students to solve it. You may want to tell them that a cup is about 250 mL just for a sense of scale.

- When would you ever want to make juice for fifty people?

- Do you think you could lift that much juice?

- About how much is that in liters?

Haunted Purple

This one is designed to have the numbers work out easily, even though there are fractional cans involved. You can probe understanding in debriefing with questions such as,

- What if you had to use two cans of Gooey Grape? Then what would you add to make three liters of Haunted Purple? (Trick question. It's impossible.) So what's the smallest amount of Haunted Purple you can make if you start with two liters of Gooey Grape?

Students can use manipulatives to help them with this problem. See what they do and ask them about it in debriefing. Do any groups use *one* block to stand for *half* a can?

Juice Mixup 1 and 2

These are complex proportion problems in which you mix strong and weak orange juice to make orange juice that's just right. The second is harder in that it's specific and uses particular measurements and limited quantities; in the first, you have an inexhaustible supply and deal only with ratios.

In the first, you can use manipulatives (such as blocks), though you have to be careful what they stand for. It helps, for example, to use one color of blocks for water and another for frozen juice. See what your students do; their solution may be better than ours. In the *Juice Mixup 2*, you have to deal with the deliciously arcane interrelationship of fluid ounces and gallons (though the relationship is stated in the clues and the numbers work out pretty well).

The first is workable at sixth grade, the second, not before seventh.

▲ Juice for Fifty

One can of frozen orange juice is 12 ounces.

How many pitchers will you need if you make juice for fifty people?

▼ Juice for Fifty

You're helping to organize a huge breakfast for the whole class and their families. You think fifty people will show up, and each one will drink about 8 ounces (one cup) of orange juice.

How many cans of water will you need?

◄ Juice for Fifty

A can of frozen orange juice costs $1.19. You mix it with three cans of water to make orange juice.

How many cans of frozen orange juice will you need for fifty people?

► Juice for Fifty

Your friends bring half-gallon pitchers from home. A half gallon is 64 fluid ounces.

How much will it cost to make enough orange juice for fifty people?

○ Juice for Fifty

There are eight fluid ounces in a cup, and two cups in a pint.

When 12 ounces of frozen orange juice melt, 12 ounces of orange goo remain.

Extension: If you got a deal on the juice—89¢ per can, say—how much would you save?

△ Juice for Fifty

There are two pints in a quart, and four quarts in a gallon.

Some people will drink less than eight ounces, but you know there will be some real juice-guzzlers at your breakfast, so eight ounces per person is a good estimate.

from *United We Solve*

copyright © 1996 by eeps media

Number, juice. Multiple questions.

Cluster: Mixtures

▲ Haunted Purple

Haunted Purple is a color that makes people shiver just to look at it. It makes them think of the inside of a casket—just as the lid is closing. You need three liters of Haunted Purple.

How will you make three liters of Haunted Purple?

▶ Haunted Purple

You can make Haunted Purple if you mix three cans of Velvet Violet and two cans of Abyss Blue with one of Midnight Black.

Every can in this problem holds one liter of paint.

◀ Haunted Purple

If you mix one can of Velvet Violet with one of Midnight Black, you get Gooey Grape.

How many liters of which colors should you mix to make the Haunted Purple that you need?

▶ Haunted Purple

You have one liter of Gooey Grape that you have to use up as you make Haunted Purple.

How many liters of Velvet Violet, Abyss Blue, and Midnight Black should you add to the Gooey Grape to make the paint you need?

○ Haunted Purple

How many liters of which colors should you mix to make the Haunted Purple that you need?

Hint: To make your paint the correct color, the overall ratio of Velvet Violet to Abyss Blue to Midnight Black has to be the same as in the recipe for Haunted Purple.

△ Haunted Purple

There is some Gooey Grape already mixed, so think about the colors that went into it as you calculate what you need to make Haunted Purple.

How many liters of which colors should you add to the Gooey Grape to make the Haunted Purple that you need?

from *United We Solve*

Number, mixing paint.

Cluster: Mixtures

▲ Juice Mixup 1

Isabel mixed a vat of orange juice (gallons and gallons) but she made it too strong. She thought you mixed two cans of frozen juice to every three cans of water.

◄ Juice Mixup 1

The real recipe for orange juice is three cans of water to every one can of frozen orange juice.

Manipulatives—blocks or beans or paper clips, say—might be useful in solving this problem.

○ Juice Mixup 1

Hint: One way to think about this problem is to figure out what percent frozen orange juice the mixtures are. Denny's, for example, is 20% frozen orange juice.

What's Isabel's? What's regular orange juice?

▼ Juice Mixup 1

Denny mixed a vat of orange juice (gallons and gallons) but he made it too weak. He thought you mixed four cans of water to every one can of frozen orange juice.

► Juice Mixup 1

Your group must figure out how much of Isabel's mixture to mix with how much of Denny's mixture to make orange juice in the correct proportions.

In this problem, it doesn't matter how much you make as long as it tastes right.

△ Juice Mixup 1

You will need more of the weak mixture—Denny's—than the strong—Isabel's—to get it to come out right.

from *United We Solve*

copyright © 1996 by eeps media

Number, juice.

Cluster: Mixtures

Juice Mixup 2

Your little brother Jake is helping you make orange juice for the Giant Family Breakfast. He brings you a gallon of what looks like orange juice. You taste it—a tiny bit.

"This is too strong, Jake!" you say. "How many cans of frozen juice did you put in?"

"Four," he says, "I thought it was one per quart. Then I just filled it up."

Juice Mixup 2

Your cousin Esmerelda is helping you make orange juice for the Giant Family Breakfast. She brings you a gallon of what looks like orange juice. You taste it—a tiny bit.

"This is too weak, Esme," you say. "How many cans of frozen juice did you put in?"

"I thought it was one can per half gallon," she says "I put in two and then filled it up."

Juice Mixup 2

The real recipe for orange juice is three cans of water to every one can of frozen orange juice. It makes four cans of juice.

You need orange juice for the breakfast, and you have only Jake's and Esme's gallons. No water, no more frozen juice.

A quart is two pints, and a pint is 16 fluid ounces.

Juice Mixup 2

A can of frozen juice is 12 fluid ounces. A gallon is four quarts.

Your group has to figure out the most juice you can make by mixing Esme's and Jake's juice together—and have it be the right proportions. There may be some part of somebody's mixture left over.

Juice Mixup 2

Hint: If you just pour Esme's and Jake's gallons together, you'll have two gallons. But what's it made of? It's 72 ounces (six cans of frozen juice at 12 ounces per can) in 256 ounces (2 gallons at 128 ounces per gallon) of mix.

That's not the right proportion. Think about whether that mix is too strong or too weak.

Juice Mixup 2

Hint: This problem might be hard to do with manipulatives. You might have to think about ratios of frozen juice to water, or frozen juice to the mix.

For example, in regular juice, the frozen juice is 25% of the mix, or the ratio of juice to water is 1 : 3.

from *United We Solve*

Number, juice. POW.

Cluster: Mixtures

Rates

Materials: scratch paper, pencils, calculators

Math: number, proportion

These problems are about rates: the way things change with time. Simple rate problems tend not to have four pieces of information (The car is going 75 kilometers per hour; it's 110 kilometers to Langley; how long will it take to get there?). These problems are by nature more complex. There may be two rates and we see when the quantities are equal; we may compare different rates to see which is fastest; there may be different rates at different times to be put together.

Dog Years

How old is Sadie? This is a twist on the old, "Marianne is twice as old now as her brother was four years ago" problems, except that Sadie is a dog, and some of the ages are in dog years. In this problem, one person year is six dog years. Your students may disagree; that's OK. See clue ○.

- How did you organize your information to keep track of it?

Fester & the Nunz

Francesca shaves her head, and later her brother gets most of his hair cut off. When will their hair be the same length? How long will it be? (Note: two questions) Their hair grows at different rates. Watch to see how students organize their thinking. Do they use a table? A graph? Anything?

- (During) How many months is it between Halloween and New Year's Eve?

- How did you organize your thinking in this problem?

- Does hair really grow at that rate? How would you know how fast hair grows?

Triple Crown

A problem for the horse-crazy. In which of the the 1973 Triple Crown races did Secretariat run the fastest on the average? Students need to be clear that speed is not the same as short duration, and clue ◄ should help them with that.

In one way, the question is unanswerable because the clues do not define *average* speed (What if the horse ran *really* fast for a little while and then much slower…). In field-test, however, that was not confusing, and so we left the issue out entirely to keep the verbiage down. If it comes up, you can deal with it by defining average speed as the whole distance divided by the whole time.

Don't miss clue ➤ about what the "decimal" point means in horse-racing times.

- How do you allow for the different distances?

- (Extension) How would you change Secretariat's speed to miles per hour?

Skyhawk 9792H

How much gas will you need to fly from Las Vegas to Bakersfield? This is a genuine, to-scale, aviation calculation. You have to deal with two rates: how fast you travel, and how fast you use up gasoline.

- Have you ever been in a light plane?

- Do you know how much gas a car's gas tank holds?

- How long is a statute mile? (Note: many airplanes in metric countries use *nautical* miles.)

- How did you decide whether to stop in Palmdale?

Dog Years

Some people say that one person-year is six dog-years. So that if a dog is three person-years old, the dog is 18 dog-years old.

How old is Sadie?

Dog Years

Chelsea and Sadie are dogs. Dwight is their boy.

Chelsea is twice as many dog-years old right now as Dwight is person-years old.

How old is Sadie?

Dog Years

Dwight goes to Taylor Middle School. Chelsea and Sadie are his dogs.

Chelsea was born on Dwight's eighth birthday.

How old is Sadie?

Dog Years

Sadie is Chelsea's best friend. She's a dog, too.

Sadie's age in person-years is one-third Chelsea's age in dog-years.

How old is Sadie?

Dog Years

Hint: Keeping track of person-years and dog-years can be confusing. A table might help.

Extension: Some people say that there are seven dog-years for every person-year. Would that change this problem?

Dog Years

Hint: A table or a chart might help you figure out this problem.

Extension: Here's another question you might be able to answer: Was Chelsea ever the same age in dog-years as Dwight was in person-years?

from United We Solve

Ages, time. Organizing information.

Cluster: Rates

▲ Fester & the Nunz

For Halloween, Francesca decided to go as Uncle Fester (the bald guy on *The Addams Family*). On a dare, she shaved off all her hair. She had none left. None. Zip. Zilch. You could use her head for a globe.

It was a great costume, but she wore a hat for weeks.

▼ Fester & the Nunz

When will Francesca's hair be the same length as Nuncio's?

Francesca's hair grows 12 mm per month.

◄ Fester & the Nunz

It was a bad hair year for Francesca and her family.

Nuncio's haircut actually took place on New Year's Eve. His hair grows faster than Francesca's: 16 mm per month.

How long will his hair be when it's the same length as Francesca's?

► Fester & the Nunz

Francesca's little brother Nuncio ("the Nunz") is in first grade. Five years old. Over the Winter break, he decided to give himself a haircut. It was a disaster.

They hoped it would grow out in time, but before he went back to school on January 2, they had to cut his hair off, leaving only 6 mm.

○ Fester & the Nunz

There are two questions your group has to answer:

When will Francesca's hair be the same length as the Nunz's? and

How long will it be then?

Remember: *Distance = Rate × Time.*

△ Fester & the Nunz

Hint: One approach to this problem is to make a chart. You could also make a graph.

According to some barbers we talked to, 12 mm is typical, while 16 mm per month is pretty fast. How fast do you think your hair grows?

from *United We Solve*

copyright © 1996 by eeps media

Length, growth.

Cluster: Rates

Triple Crown

In 1973, Secretariat (a horse) won the Kentucky Derby with a time of 1:59.2.

The Belmont Stakes is a one and one-half mile race.

In which Triple Crown race did Secretariat run the fastest in 1973?

Triple Crown

In 1973, Secretariat won the Preakness Stakes with a time of 1:54.2.

The Kentucky Derby is one and one-quarter miles long.

The other "Triple Crown" race is the Belmont Stakes. Secretariat won all three.

Triple Crown

In 1973, Secretariat won the Belmont Stakes with a time of 2:24.0.

The Preakness Stakes is a one and three-sixteenths mile race.

Even though Secretariat's time for the Preakness was the shortest, it may not have been the one in which he ran the fastest.

Triple Crown

In Thoroughbred racing, the time for a race is given in minutes, seconds, and *fifths* of a second, even though the last part is after a decimal point.

So 1:33.4 means one minute, thirty-three seconds, and four fifths (not four tenths) of a second. That's 93.8 seconds altogether.

Triple Crown

Even though Secretariat's time for the Belmont Stakes is the longest, it was not his slowest race. It was the farthest he had to run, so of course it took longer—even though he ran faster than in a shorter race.

In which race did he run the fastest?

Triple Crown

Hint: You can think about speed by the way we talk about it—in miles per hour, say. In a horse race, you will probably want to use seconds, not hours. So you can (for example) compute seconds per mile or miles per second. Which one is a speed?

Hint: *Distance = Speed × Time*, so what does *Speed* equal?

171

from *United We Solve*

Measurement, distance, speed.

Cluster: Rates

▲ Skyhawk 9792H

9792H (you say, "niner seven niner two hotel.") is a single-engine plane—a Cessna 172 "Skyhawk," built in 1974. You're about to fly it from Las Vegas, Nevada, to Bakersfield, California. A good route takes you over Palmdale.

Your plane's gas tanks hold 38 gallons.

▼ Skyhawk 9792H

It's about 195 (statute) miles from Las Vegas (McCarran International Airport, elevation 2175 feet) to the Palmdale airport.

You should probably make this trip at 8500 feet altitude.

How much gas will you need for your flight? Will you have to stop in Palmdale?

◄ Skyhawk 9792H

At 7,500 feet, the Cessna 172 will go 126 miles per hour (mph) while burning 7.1 gallons per hour; if you speed up to 133 mph, it will burn 7.6 gallons per hour.

Climbing from sea level to 10,000 feet requires between three and five gallons of fuel depending on the weight in the plane.

► Skyhawk 9792H

It's about 80 miles from the Palmdale airport to Bakersfield's Meadows Field.

At 10,000 feet, the Cessna 172 will burn 6.8 gallons of gas per hour if you go 124 miles per hour (mph); if you go 131 mph, you will burn 7.3 gallons per hour.

○ Skyhawk 9792H

You don't have all of the information you need to solve this problem, but you can make some pretty good guesses.

One is that you can ignore the fuel you need to come down. It doesn't take any extra fuel at all to descend!

△ Skyhawk 9792H

Distance = Speed × Time, but also,

Gas Used = Rate × Time.

Extension: Calculate how long the flight takes. Figure that while you climb you're only going 80 mph and that the climb takes 20 minutes.

172

from *United We Solve*

copyright © 1996 by eeps media

Consumption rates. Multiple questions. POW.

Cluster: Rates

Product Chains

Materials: scratch paper, pencils, calculators, manipulatives

Math: generalizing from patterns, compound proportions, formulas

The point of these problems is to generalize. Groups may construct tables or formulas as they see fit according to the directions. But *you* may have a different agenda. For example, you may want to insist on formulas. If so, simply do that orally and don't pass out clue △, which explicitly gives permission for a variety of methods.

Food Chain

In this problem, students must figure out how many of the animals at the bottom of the food chain (dorblotts) they need to support *any* number of the ones at the top (rodelians). Clue ➤ suggests *seven* rodelians as an example, but the clues clearly ask for a generalization. That can take the form of a formula, a table, a graph, or anything that gets the job done.

- Suppose we had fifty rodelians. How many dorblotts would we need? How did you figure that out?

- Why don't you have to figure out the number of quigs every time?

Food Chain 2

This is like *Food Chain* but backwards. Given a number of creatures at the bottom (snortiblasts), find the number of the ones at the top (gronks) they will support. Students will have to deal with remainders.

- How did your group deal with left over snortiblasts?

Basketballs

How many basketballs does the district need, given *any* number of middle schools?

- How do you think they really figure out how many basketballs to buy?

Rats and Mice

How many mice are in the town—given the number of rats? Clues relate mice to cats, rats to dogs, and cats and dogs to households. In this problem, the constant of proportionality is not an integer.

- What do you know about the number of rats in the town? Could there be twelve rats?
  (No. It has to be a multiple of five.)

Food Chain

Rodelians feed every night. Each rodelian eats five snoppits.

You work at the zoo. They're thinking of bringing in some rodelians and they want to know how many dorblotts they will need to keep the rodelians alive.

Food Chain

Snoppits feed every night. Each snoppit eats three quigs.

The zoo people want to know the number of dorblotts they'll need, but they aren't concerned about the pipworts and quigs and snoppits.

Food Chain

Quigs feed every night. Each quig eats twelve pipworts.

You and your group need to come up with a scheme for calculating the number of dorblotts you'll need. It should be easy for the zoo director to use your scheme with any number of rodelians.

Food Chain

Pipworts feed every night. Each pipwort eats four dorblotts.

Your job, with your group, is to come up with a way to calculate the number of dorblotts the zoo will need each night for any number of rodelians, for example, seven.

Food Chain

Hint: One way to test your scheme is to see if it works if there is only one rodelian, or two.

Does your scheme work for zero rodelians?

Food Chain

Hint: There are a number of ways to solve this problem. You might make a table, or an equation, or a graph, or some other way.

Any method is OK as long as the zoo directors can figure the number of dorblotts easily.

from *United We Solve*

Algebra, generalizing, constants of proprtionality.

Cluster: Product Chains

Food Chain 2

Gronks feed every night. Each gronk eats two torfs.

You work at the zoo. They're thinking of bringing in some gronks and they want to know how many they can support given any number of snortiblasts.

This problem is something like the one called Food Chain.

Food Chain 2

Torfs feed every night. Each torf eats six jynkos.

The zoo people want to know the number of gronks they can support, but right now they aren't concerned about the jynkos and torfs and umies.

Food Chain 2

Jynkos feed every night. Each jynko eats five umies.

You and your group need to come up with a scheme for calculating the number of gronks you can support. It should be easy for the zoo director to use your scheme with any number of snortiblasts.

Food Chain 2

Umies feed every night. Each umie eats ten teeny snortiblasts.

Your job, with your group, is to come up with a way to calculate the number of gronks the zoo can support each night for any number of snortiblasts, for example, 1800 or 750.

Food Chain 2

Hint: You may want to start by making a table.

One way to test your scheme is to see if it works if there is enough for one gronk.

There may be a problem with remainders: What should you do if there are enough snortiblasts for, say, two and a half gronks?

Food Chain 2

Hint: There are a number of ways to solve this problem. You might make a table, or an equation, or a graph, or some other way.

Any method is OK as long as the zoo directors can figure the number of gronks easily.

from *United We Solve*

Algebra, generalizing, constants of proprtionality.

Cluster: Product Chains

Basketballs

Every middle school in the district has 24 classrooms.

Your job, with your group, is to come up with a way to figure out how many basketballs the district needs.

Basketballs

Each classroom in the district has 30 students.

Work with your group to figure out how many basketballs the district needs. Your way should work for any number of middle schools, for example, three.

Basketballs

At any time, only one-sixth of all students are taking P.E.

Your scheme for figuring out how many basketballs you need should be easy to explain for any number of schools, for example, five.

One way to show your scheme is with a formula.

Basketballs

The P.E. Program needs one basketball for every ten students who are playing.

How many basketballs does the district need? Devise a way to figure it out that works for any number of schools. Anything is OK as long as it works and it's clear.

Basketballs

Hint: One way to test your final scheme (you did test it, didn't you?) is to see if it works with only one school in the district. Then try it with two.

Extension: Is your scheme a reasonable way to decide the number of basketballs for a real school?

Basketballs

Hint: There are a number of ways to solve this problem. You might make a table, or an equation, or a graph, or some other way.

Any method is OK as long as the school people can figure the number of basketballs easily.

from *United We Solve*

copyright © 1996 by eeps media

Algebra, generalizing, constants of proprtionality.

Cluster: Product Chains

Rats & Mice

How many mice are in the town?

For every dog in the town, there are five rats.

Work with your group. Come up with a way to calculate the number of mice if you know the number of rats.

Rats & Mice

For every cat in the town, there are eight mice.

Work with your group to come up with a way to calculate the number of mice if you know the number of rats. Your scheme should work for many different numbers of rats, for example, 255.

Rats & Mice

Every house in the town has two cats and one dog.

Work with your group to come up with a way to calculate the number of mice if you know the number of rats. Your scheme should work for many different numbers of rats, for example, 100.

Rats & Mice

There are no stray cats or dogs in the town: every cat and every dog lives in a house with people.

How many mice are in the town?

Work with your group. Come up with a way to calculate the number of mice if you know the number of rats.

Rats & Mice

Hint: One way to test your method (you did test it, didn't you?) is to see if it works with only one house in the town. Then try it with two.

Extension: There are some numbers of rats that don't work in this problem. How can you tell whether a number will work or not?

Rats & Mice

Hint: There are a number of ways to solve this problem. You might make a table, or an equation, or a graph, or some other display.

Any method is OK as long as the you can figure the number of mice easily.

from *United We Solve*

Algebra, generalizing, constants of proprtionality.

Cluster: Product Chains

Inaccessible Distances

Materials: scratch paper, graph paper, pencils, rulers, calculators

Math: proportion, similarity

Each group member has part of the situation or a measurement to help the group solve a problem about measuring inaccessible distances. All of these problems have to do with similar triangles and proportion, though they differ in what part of the triangle the students have to solve for.

For example, if you know the distance to a building and its apparent height, you can derive its actual height. If, on the other hand, you know its actual height, you can derive its distance.

There is a place in many curricula where students measure things by pacing them off and calibrating their paces. These problems are good to do at that time.

Distant Train

Note: there is a common clue that everyone should read and discuss before they look at their individual clues.

How far away was the train? Dwayne and Penelope are trying to figure it out, but they only have Dwayne's pocket comb to measure with. When they get to the station, the train hasn't left yet, so they can figure out the actual size of the train by pacing it off. Groups need to set up a number of proportions and similar triangles, though they don't have to know those terms.

- What pictures did you draw to help you?

- How far away is that? As far as the road? Farther than from here to your house (or whatever is appropriate)?

Poisonacid River

How far is it across the river? This problem is a little different from the others in that it's not about measuring things with rulers at arm's length and using proportions. Instead, it's what in high school would be a trigonometry problem. One good way for middle-schoolers and pre-trig kids to solve it is to make a scale drawing—and that's where the proportion comes in.

- Show me your picture of what's happening in the situation. What do you know based on the picture?

- What's the scale in your picture?

Old Needledropper

How tall is that tree? Instead of the old shadow technique, Zoltan and Tonya use rulers held at arm's length.

- Is that a reasonable height for a tree?

- Why don't you have to know the length of Tonya's arm?

- What picture did you draw to help you?

The Plaque

How far is it from the flagpole to the plaque? In *Old Needledropper*, the inaccessible distance was the height. Here the inaccessible distance is between the tall object (the flagpole) and the observer (who is at the plaque).

This problem is in English units. Students need to know that one foot is twelve inches.

- Why does Jared need Tonya's help? Could he do it without her?

- How do you show the relationship between Tonya and the flagpole in a picture?

- What proportions do you use to find the distance? Why do they make sense?

▲ Distant Train

In ten paces, Dwayne goes 9.2 meters (he remembered this from an activity at school).

They counted the cars at the station. There were twelve.

How far away was the train?

Which information is unnecessary?

▼ Distant Train

Dwayne's pocket comb is 20 cm long.

Dwayne paced off one of the cars. It was 24 paces long.

How far away was the train?

Which information is unnecessary?

◄ Distant Train

Dwayne went to the middle of one car and paced off 24 paces perpendicular to the car. He found himself at the pay phone.

Extra question: What assumptions do you have to make to figure out the distance to the train?

► Distant Train

When Penelope measured the car from the pay phone, it appeared to be five times as long as the comb.

The twelve cars were all identical.

How far away was the train?

Which information is unnecessary?

❖ Distant Train

Read this problem situation and discuss it. Then look at your own cards and answer the questions.

Dwayne and Penelope were riding their bikes along the old county road when they saw a passenger train away across the valley, heading into town.

Penelope borrowed Dwayne's pocket comb and held it at arm's length. The train (without the engine) appeared to be half as long as the comb.

They wondered how far away the train was. They knew they didn't have enough information to figure it out, so when they got into town, they went to the station. The train was there.

All of your individual cards are about their measurements at the station.

How far away was the train? Which information is unnecessary?

from *United We Solve*

Geometry, measurement, proportion. Multiple questions. POW.   **Cluster: Inaccessible Distances**

▲ Poisonacid River

Dan, Vicky, Mike, and Charlene are trying to figure out how wide the Poisonacid River is. They can't cross it—it's too dangerous.

Dan stands directly across from a tall cedar tree they see on the opposite bank. He uses his compass. The tree is due north.

▼ Poisonacid River

Where they are, the Poisonacid River runs east and west.

Mike paces 21 steps from where Dan is standing to where Charlene is standing.

Your group will probably need a protractor and a ruler for this problem.

◄ Poisonacid River

Charlene is standing on the south bank of the Poisonacid River helping her friends figure out how wide it is.

When Charlene uses her compass, she sees that the cedar tree opposite Dan is 30° west of north from her. That is, the angle between north and the direction to the tree is 30°.

► Poisonacid River

Dan, Vicky, Mike, and Charlene are trying to figure out how wide the Poisonacid River is. They can't cross it—it's too dangerous.

Vicky measured 5 of Mike's paces with a five-meter tape. Altogether, they were 4.6 meters.

○ Poisonacid River

Hint: Unless you know trigonometry, your group will probably need to make a scale drawing to solve this problem.

Check: is the distance you get a reasonable width for a river? Is it wider than a street? Wider than the length of a football field?

△ Poisonacid River

Extension and a check: how far is it from where Charlene is standing to the cedar tree? How does that compare with the distance from Charlene to Dan? (It should be twice the distance.)

Can you explain why it should be exactly twice the distance?

from *United We Solve*

copyright © 1996 by eeps media

Geometry, measurement, angles, compass directions. POW.   **Cluster: Inaccessible Distances**

▲ Old Needledropper

Tonya's friend Zoltan is 175 cm tall.

Old Needledropper is a huge pine tree at Taylor Middle School.

Your group's job is to figure out how tall it is. It helps to draw a picture or diagram.

▼ Old Needledropper

Tonya had Zoltan stand 100 of her paces from the base of Old Needledropper. Then she went thirteen paces more and turned around to measure Zoltan and the tree.

How tall is Old Needledropper?

◄ Old Needledropper

From where Tonya is standing, her friend Zoltan looks to be 19 cm tall—measured with a meter stick held at arm's length.

How tall is Old Needledropper?

► Old Needledropper

From where Tonya is standing, Old Needledropper appears to be 33 cm tall. That's taller than Zoltan appears to be.

How tall is Old Needledropper, the huge pine tree?

○ Old Needledropper

Tonya measured her pace as 82 cm. She decided she didn't need to measure the length of her arm as long as she made all her measurements the same way.

Extension: Did she need to know the length of her pace?

△ Old Needledropper

Hint: In problems like these, it sometimes helps to imagine things that are not in the problem, for example, a smaller tree ("Young Needledropper") that appears to be the same size as Zoltan but is at the same distance as Old Needledropper.

from *United We Solve*

181

Geometry, measurement, proportion. POW.

Cluster: Inaccessible Distances

The Plaque

Previous generations of students have measured Taylor Middle School's flagpole. Everybody knows it's 42 feet tall.

But how far is it from the flagpole to the plaque?

The Plaque

Jared is measuring the distance from the flagpole to the plaque set into the school's front steps. He gets his friend Tonya (who stands 5 feet 4 inches tall) to help.

He kneels down and rests his head on the plaque to make his measurement.

The Plaque

To make his measurement, Jared directs his friend Tonya to stand so that she appears to be exactly the height of the flagpole. That is, her feet look lined up with the bottom and her head looks lined up with the top.

There are twelve inches in one foot.

The Plaque

While Tonya stands where Jared has asked her to stand, Jared measures the distance from Tonya's feet to the plaque. It's 11 feet 6 inches.

How far is it from the plaque to the flagpole?

The Plaque

Jared—with his head on the pavement—directs Tonya to the right place by saying stuff like, "a little back…a little to your left…there." A few people look at them funny, but mostly they're used to this at Taylor Middle School.

Jared's measuring tape is only 12 feet long.

The Plaque

There's a thick thorn hedge between the flagpole and the plaque that keeps Jared from measuring the distance directly.

You can't read the plaque anymore. Students at Taylor Middle School call the plaque "the Tomb of the Unknown Teacher," or "TUT."

from *United We Solve*

copyright © 1996 by eeps media

Geometry, measurement, proportion. POW.

Cluster: Inaccessible Distances

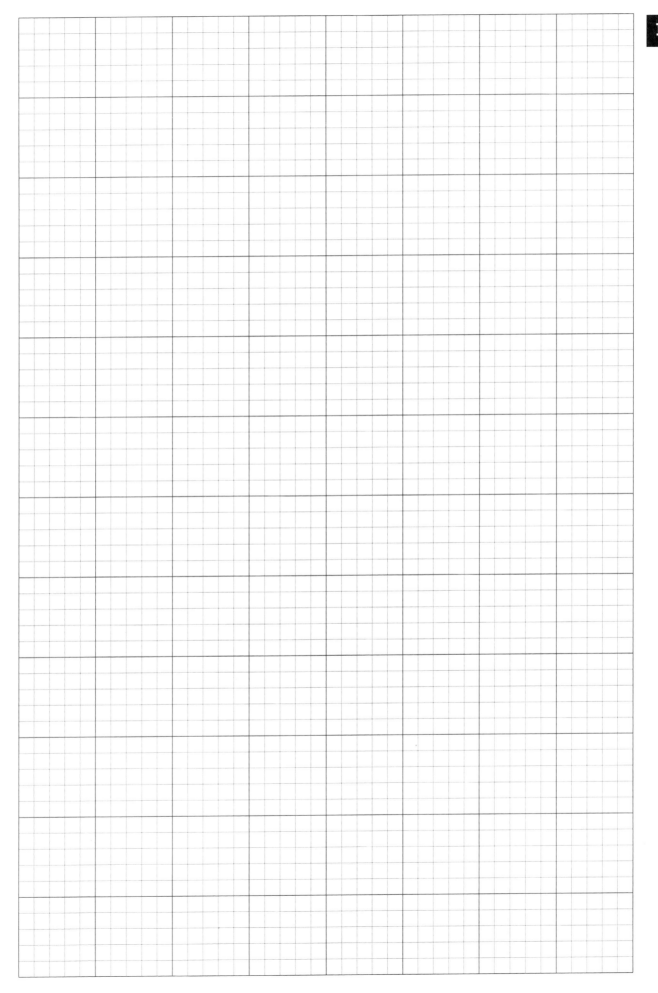

United States Map

HAWAII

CALIFORNIA

OREGON

WASHINGTON

ALASKA

NEVADA

IDAHO

ARIZONA

UTAH

MONTANA

NEW MEXICO

COLORADO

WYOMING

SOUTH DAKOTA

NORTH DAKOTA

TEXAS

OKLAHOMA

KANSAS

NEBRASKA

IOWA

MINNESOTA

LOUISIANA

ARKANSAS

MISSOURI

ILLINOIS

WISCONSIN

Lake Superior

MISSISSIPPI

ALABAMA

TENNESSEE

KENTUCKY

INDIANA

MICHIGAN

Lake Michigan

Lake Huron

GEORGIA

SOUTH CAROLINA

NORTH CAROLINA

VIRGINIA

WEST VIRGINIA

OHIO

Lake Erie

Lake Ontario

PENNSYLVANIA

NEW YORK

VERMONT

MAINE

FLORIDA

Washington D.C.

MARYLAND

DELAWARE

NEW JERSEY

CONNECTICUT

RHODE ISLAND

MASSACHUSETTS

NEW HAMPSHIRE

This table presents data from the 1990 U.S. Census. These are just a few of the many variables.

	About the population						Median Household Income	About households with kids under 18		
	Total Population	Black	Asian	Hispanic	Age 85+	Prisoners		Single Mother	Single Father	Two parents
Alabama	4,040,587	1,019,743	21,754	23,579	47,844	19,109	$23,597	106,279	16,644	406,907
Alaska	550,043	22,195	19,354	17,904	1,110	2,694	$41,408	13,321	4,824	65,058
Arizona	3,665,228	110,062	54,127	680,628	36,802	21,873	$27,540	85,385	24,875	344,302
Arkansas	2,350,725	373,454	12,098	19,586	34,707	8,699	$21,147	55,835	10,579	243,917
California	29,760,021	2,198,766	2,847,835	7,557,550	288,445	177,949	$35,798	661,698	200,612	2,752,645
Colorado	3,294,394	131,223	59,411	419,322	32,528	13,181	$30,140	79,453	19,094	343,454
Connecticut	3,287,116	273,555	48,962	203,511	45,707	9,830	$41,721	71,720	12,214	307,991
Delaware	666,168	112,125	8,770	15,151	6,959	3,398	$34,875	14,692	3,403	64,482
District of Columbia	606,900	399,751	11,233	31,358	7,706	4,221	$30,727	24,012	3,067	23,983
Florida	12,937,926	1,755,958	150,200	1,555,031	205,586	78,523	$27,483	292,238	69,389	1,082,110
Georgia	6,478,216	1,744,882	73,757	101,379	55,622	42,354	$29,021	184,292	31,039	650,526
Hawaii	1,108,229	26,669	686,391	78,742	10,669	2,570	$38,829	16,895	5,647	104,488
Idaho	1,006,749	3,653	9,096	51,679	10,969	2,783	$25,257	18,597	5,762	113,964
Illinois	11,430,602	1,690,855	284,944	878,682	143,159	36,424	$32,252	271,242	52,437	1,101,392
Indiana	5,544,159	429,722	36,595	95,363	69,502	21,905	$28,797	125,022	28,493	578,439
Iowa	2,776,755	47,259	24,325	30,642	54,401	5,628	$26,229	52,167	11,964	294,294
Kansas	2,477,574	141,957	31,114	90,289	41,888	11,302	$27,291	50,553	11,821	268,149
Kentucky	3,685,296	262,057	17,309	20,363	44,064	14,356	$22,534	86,390	16,538	400,783
Louisiana	4,219,973	1,298,662	39,675	90,609	41,584	26,577	$21,949	136,643	22,442	414,801
Maine	1,227,928	5,351	6,859	7,069	17,844	2,376	$27,854	26,475	6,881	129,599
Maryland	4,781,468	1,188,930	137,663	119,984	45,329	27,469	$39,386	120,057	24,740	449,703
Massachusetts	6,016,425	297,006	140,745	275,859	89,791	15,661	$36,952	137,388	20,636	540,884
Michigan	9,295,297	1,289,012	102,869	189,915	105,769	43,207	$31,020	262,827	47,054	899,097
Minnesota	4,375,099	94,798	76,771	49,664	66,305	10,367	$30,909	86,577	20,893	470,811
Mississippi	2,573,216	915,858	12,706	14,745	31,736	8,525	$20,136	83,073	12,838	249,436
Missouri	5,117,073	546,850	39,580	60,429	81,057	20,032	$26,362	119,792	23,739	516,877
Montana	799,065	2,047	4,256	12,167	10,506	2,234	$22,988	17,595	4,845	86,022
Nebraska	1,578,385	57,128	12,566	35,093	28,413	3,773	$26,016	31,361	6,893	171,771
Nevada	1,201,833	78,310	38,053	121,346	7,305	8,457	$31,011	27,955	9,450	109,429
New Hampshire	1,109,252	7,155	9,035	11,558	12,653	1,968	$36,329	19,407	5,772	122,006
New Jersey	7,730,188	1,035,386	269,808	720,344	92,962	30,323	$40,927	153,802	32,734	728,225
New Mexico	1,515,069	29,818	14,372	576,709	13,305	5,693	$24,087	39,071	13,667	157,439
New York	17,990,455	2,860,590	689,262	2,151,743	241,541	90,341	$32,965	470,215	82,905	1,554,039
North Carolina	6,628,637	1,455,340	50,395	69,020	68,857	25,229	$26,647	164,000	31,588	652,007
North Dakota	638,800	3,519	3,184	4,658	11,152	908	$23,213	11,327	2,651	72,716
Ohio	10,847,115	1,152,230	89,238	131,983	137,099	42,146	$28,706	270,002	51,271	1,083,791
Oklahoma	3,145,585	232,244	32,561	83,654	43,948	15,728	$23,577	74,167	15,817	332,636
Oregon	2,842,321	45,423	67,641	110,606	37,122	12,056	$27,250	62,789	19,549	277,553
Pennsylvania	11,881,643	1,087,570	135,096	220,479	168,039	43,946	$29,069	238,716	51,934	1,112,522
Rhode Island	1,003,464	37,986	17,615	43,932	15,916	2,900	$32,181	22,497	4,231	91,503
South Carolina	3,486,703	1,040,010	21,298	28,334	29,457	19,024	$26,256	94,241	16,365	344,292
South Dakota	696,004	3,133	3,327	5,428	13,411	2,546	$22,503	13,342	3,428	76,699
Tennessee	4,877,185	777,041	30,595	31,075	57,748	21,534	$24,807	123,819	21,988	489,552
Texas	16,986,510	2,018,543	315,072	4,294,120	162,035	95,293	$27,016	407,085	88,835	1,811,915
Utah	1,722,850	11,079	33,000	83,097	13,532	4,229	$29,470	31,632	6,986	206,801
Vermont	562,758	2,194	3,064	3,862	7,291	745	$29,792	12,264	3,686	59,000
Virginia	6,187,358	1,163,068	158,808	155,353	58,385	32,029	$33,328	133,401	28,058	626,405
Washington	4,866,692	147,364	211,292	206,018	55,153	14,777	$31,183	111,190	30,774	490,703
West Virginia	1,793,477	55,398	7,505	7,892	24,130	4,420	$20,795	36,673	8,514	191,544
Wisconsin	4,891,769	244,305	53,058	87,609	71,900	13,698	$29,442	106,230	22,925	504,192
Wyoming	453,588	3,290	2,742	24,976	4,385	1,590	$27,096	9,743	2,915	53,263

Notes: *Hispanic* does not exclude any other categories: you can be both Black and Hispanic. *Asian* means "Asian and Pacific Islanders." *Prisoners* means, "Living as an inmate in a correctional institution." In "households with kids under 18," at least one of the children is a child (not grandchild, niece, etc.) of a parent. Visit http://www.eeps.com to download these data.

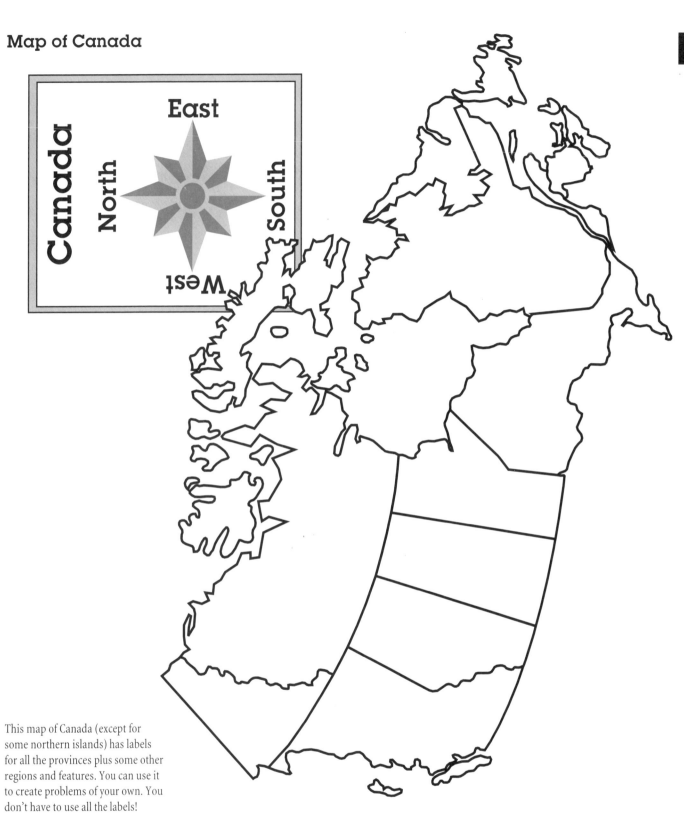

This map of Canada (except for some northern islands) has labels for all the provinces plus some other regions and features. You can use it to create problems of your own. You don't have to use all the labels!

Labrador	Victoria Island		Hudson Bay
Baffin Island	District of Mackenzie		District of Keewatin
New Brunswick	Alberta	Manitoba	Newfoundland
British Columbia	Yukon	Nova Scotia	◄ Prince Edward Island
Saskatchewan	Ontario	Québec	Northwest Territories

Problem and Keyword Index

Titles of problems have page numbers in **boldface**.

We hope you can use *United We Solve* to enhance whatever mathematics curriculum you use. If you use a standard textbook, you can find appropriate problems by browsing, by using the topics grid on page 192, or by using the keyword index on pages 188–189. We have not covered every topic—this volume is weak in probability and in estimation, to give two examples—but you should be able to find problems appropriate to most curriculum areas.

These two pages are for those adventurous teachers and schools who use the new, unit-based curricula that have been under development for the middle grades and for high school since about 1988. Some are available; others are in the process of being published as this book goes to press.

The curricula are exciting, and these problems were made with the spirit and the high standards of these curricula in mind.

How would you use these problems with a unit-based curriculum?

- To provide a familiar format to get students used to working together.

- With an easier problem, to introduce a concept for a unit.

- With a harder problem, to pose a "framing" problem for a unit or to pose a culminating problem.

- To inject material from another area of mathematics into the flow of a unit.

Here we present a *tentative* "correlation" between *some* of the units and the clusters of problems in this book. These are only the obvious connections; you should still browse. Many of our field testers use some of these units and speak from experience, but there hasn't been the time to do a comprehensive cross-test.

Please send your suggestions to us (see page 7) and see the updated correlations on the worldwide web!

Investigations

EQUALS Program, Lawrence Hall of Science (already available Fall 1995)

These units were originally designed for eighth grade, though some have been used at seventh. The author's association with EQUALS and Investigations shows up here: the five clusters listed were in fact inspired by these units.

Growth Patterns
Growth

Remote Rulers
Inaccessible Distances

Telling Someone Where to Go
Directions

Scatter Matters
Can You Relate?

Flea-Sized Surgeons
Pyramid Schemes

Sixth Through Eighth Mathematics (STEM)

McDougal/Littell/Houghton Mifflin

Its developers, at the University of Montana, say that STEM will be available Spring 1998. With the other projects listed here, they have been leaders in creating new middle-grades materials that reflect both a belief in student-centered learning and a commitment to serious mathematics for all.

Interactive Mathematics

Glencoe (already available Fall 1995)

Many of these units are written by the very talented David Foster. There are six units per year, grades six through eight. Not all problems in each cluster are appropriate for the grade level of the unit.

1. From the Beginning…
   This unit includes two problems from Get It Together. *Use a variety of starters.*

2. A Million to One
   Product chains; fraction-decimal problems from the Proportion category

3. Just the Right Size
   Growth, Directions, Polygons

4. Through the Looking Glass
   Arrange the Blocks

5. Get a Clue
   Maps

6. The Road Not Taken
   Networks (though they may be hard at sixth grade), Nim Games

7. Take It From the Top
   Various starters, Alien Number Systems, Mystery Operations, Moon Base

8. Data Sense
   specific problems: East & West, States and Kids; also, use census data to make up their own

9. Don't Fence Me In
   Polygons; also, A & P Graph (page 60)

10. Against the Odds
    Nim: Two Dice 21 (page 51)

11. Cycles
    Alien Number Systems, Mystery Operations

12. Treasure Island
    Round and Round, Directions

13. Start Your Engines
    Alien Number Systems, Calculator Equations

14. Run For Cover
    Pyramid Schemes

15. On the Move
    Rates, Can You Relate?

16. Growing Pains
    Growth, Can You Relate?, Inaccessible Distances

17. Infinite Windows
    Fractal Automata

18. Quality Control
    Not Enough Info, Many Faces

These projects all received NSF support, and are all forward-looking, unit-based programs. As of Spring 1997, though these three programs are almost fully available, we haven't seen final copies of all of the units. We have nevertheless made a tentative matchup for some of their units, based on outlines and drafts. We will all be better-informed after their publication. Also, not all problems in each cluster are appropriate for the grade level of the unit.

Connected Mathematics Project

Dale Seymour Publications

This 6–8 project was developed at Michigan State. Much of these materials are actually available as of Spring 1997.

Prime Time
Alien Number Systems, Mystery Operations

Shapes and Designs
Directions, Polygons

Data About Us, Data Around Us
Many Faces, Allocating Scarce Resources, Can You Relate?

Bits and Pieces (I & II)
It All Adds Up, Per, Mixtures, Rates

Covering and Surrounding
Polygons

How Likely Is It? What Do You Expect?
Nim: Two Dice 21 (page 51)

Ruins of Montarek
Arrange the Blocks

Variables and Patterns, Say It With Symbols
Product Chains (require formulas in later grades), Take It Apart

Stretching and Shrinking
Directions, Polygons (though not scale)

Accentuate the Negative
Geap (page 30), Ned & Kristin (page 25)

Comparing and Scaling
Rates, Per, It All Adds Up, Mixtures

Moving Straight Ahead
Product Chains

Filling and Wrapping
Pyramid Schemes

Variables and Patterns
Can You Relate?

Growing, Growing, Growing
Growth

Mathematics in Context

Britannica Education
email: info@ebec.com

This 5–8 project was developed at the University of Wisconsin. It comprises 40 units—10 at each grade. In general, units from their Number strand map onto this book's Proportion problems (the last 6 clusters; see the next page), and their Geometry strand can use our Spatial problems. Additional suggestions below:

This is due out by Fall 1997. Check our web site; or your favorite catalog the publisher may change.

Dry and Wet Numbers, Operations
Ned & Kristin (page 25)

Number Tools
Calculator Equations

Side Seeing
Arrange the Blocks

Figuring all the Angles
Directions (with help)

Dealing With Data, Insights Into Data
Many Faces, Can You Relate?

Expressions and Formulas, Building Formulas
Product Chains, Calculator Equations, Mystery Operations

Tracking Graphs
Can You Relate?

Packages and Polygons, Triangles and Beyond
Pyramid Schemes

Comparing Quantities
Take It Apart

Ways To Go
Networks; Round Robin (page 87)

Ups and Downs, Growth
Can You Relate?, Growth

Powers of Ten
CD-ROM (page 92), Hairy Problem (93), Directions (making scale drawings)

Digging Numbers, Reflections on Number
Alien Number Systems, Fractal Automata

Get the Most Out Of It
Take It Apart, A & P Graph (page 60)

Going the Distance
Inaccessible Distances

MathScape: Seeing and Thinking Mathematically

Creative Publications

This project comes from EDC—the Education Development Center, in Newton, Massachusetts. Available Fall 1997.

The materials already include some problems in this format.

The Language of Numbers
Alien Number Systems (In fact, just hearing about this unit inspired the cluster of problems.)

From Zero to One and Beyond, Number Powerhouse
It All Adds Up, Per

Designing Spaces
Arrange the Blocks

Gulliver's Worlds: Measuring and Scaling
Per, Directions

Buyer Beware
Per, Mixtures, Rates

Making Mathematical Arguments
Alien Number Systems

From the Ground Up
Polygons, Pyramid Schemes

The Language of Algebra
Take It Apart, Product Chains

Getting In Shape
Polygons, Round and Round

Looking Behind the Numbers
Can You Relate?

Mathematics of Motion
Rates

Shapes and Space
(pre) Arrange the Blocks

What Comes Next?
Can You Relate?, Growth

Roads and Ramps
Inaccessible Distances, Directions

Topics Grid

Legend:
- some (light)
- a lot (medium)
- the main thing (dark)

Page	Title	Number & Calculation	Logic & Language	Discrete Mathematics	Geometry	Measurement	Data & Statistics	Algebra	Functions	Rich, realistic contexts	Chance for extended work	Lowest Grade	Group
28	Alien Number Systems	main	a lot	some				a lot	some	some		5	Patterns
35	Mystery Operations	a lot	a lot	some				a lot	main			5	Patterns
41	Fractal Automata		a lot	main	some	some			a lot		some	6	Patterns
46	NIM games	some	a lot	main		some					a lot	5	Patterns
54	Can You Relate?	a lot	some		some	a lot	main	a lot	a lot	a lot	a lot	7	Patterns
61	Growth	a lot					a lot	a lot	main	a lot	a lot	8	Patterns
68	Calculator Equations	main	some	some					a lot		some	5	Open
73	Take It Apart	a lot	some					main	some			6	Open
79	Allocating Scare Resources	some	a lot	main					some	a lot	a lot	6	Open
85	Many Faces		main	some		some	some			a lot		7	Open
89	Not Enough Info!	main	a lot	some		some	some	some	a lot	a lot		7	Open
94	Networks		some	a lot						some	a lot	7	Open
100	Arrange the Blocks		a lot	some	main							5	Spatial
113	Maps		a lot	some	some	+ geography				some		6	Spatial
122	Polygons	some	some		main	a lot			some		some	6	Spatial
128	Pyramid Schemes	some	some		main			a lot	some			5	Spatial
136	Directions	some	some		main	a lot		some	some	a lot	a lot	7	Spatial
143	Round and Round	some			a lot			a lot	main	some	a lot	8	Spatial
150	It All Adds Up	main				some	some	some			a lot	5	Proportion
158	Per	main	some							some	some	5	Proportion
163	Mixtures	main	some			some		a lot	a lot	a lot	some	7	Proportion
168	Rates	a lot				a lot	some	a lot	main	a lot	a lot	7	Proportion
173	Product Chains	a lot	some					main	a lot	some	some	7	Proportion
178	Inaccessible Distances	a lot		a lot		main	some	some	a lot	some		8	Proportion